FRYDERYK CHOPIN

NOCTURNE

E♭ major / Es-Dur / Mi♭ majeur

Op. 9 No. 2

Urtext

Edited by / Herausgegeben von / Édition de

Christophe Grabowski

Editor-in-chief: John Rink

Series Editors: Jim Samson, Jean-Jacques Eigeldinger & Christophe Grabowski

Piano / Klavier

EDITION PETERS

LEIPZIG · LONDON · NEW YORK

CONTENTS

Preface v

Préface vii

Vorwort ix

NOCTURNE IN E♭ MAJOR
OP. 9 NO. 2

Page No.

(Original version)

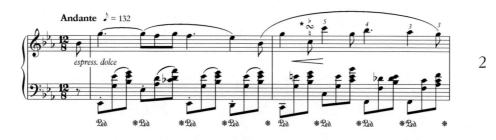

2

(Version with variants based on M²)

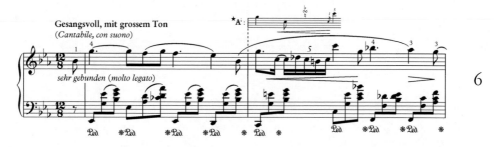

6

NOTES ON EDITORIAL METHOD AND PRACTICE 11
CRITICAL COMMENTARY 13

Nocturne Op. 9 No. 2, bars 19–34, annotated exemplar of **G¹**, PL-Tu: IV 5439 Cim.
Reproduced with kind permission of the Biblioteka Uniwersytecka w Toruniu, Gabinet Zbiorów Muzycznych.

Nocturne op. 9 n° 2, mesures 19-34, exemplaire annoté de **G¹**, PL-Tu: IV 5439 Cim.
Reproduit avec l'aimable autorisation de la Biblioteka Uniwersytecka w Toruniu, Gabinet Zbiorów Muzycznych.

Nocturne op. 9 Nr. 2, Takte 19–34, Exemplar der **G¹** mit handschriftlichen Varianten, PL-Tu: IV 5439 Cim.
Abdruck mit freundlicher Genehmigung der Biblioteka Uniwersytecka w Toruniu, Gabinet Zbiorów Muzycznych.

PREFACE

Genre and genesis

Evening, twilight and night have been sources of inspiration for countless poets, painters and musicians. In the field of music, the piano nocturne stands at the top of the list of genres evocative of the night. Before becoming one of the most emblematic manifestations of Romantic lyricism and the pure expression of *bel canto*, the title was used for pieces consisting of several movements of varied character, composed for a small instrumental ensemble and intended to enhance nightly entertainments. Examples include Joseph Haydn's eight *Notturni* Hob. II:25–32 composed for King Ferdinand IV of Naples, and Wolfgang Amadeus Mozart's *Serenata notturna* K. 239 and *Notturno* K. 286. The influence of the serenade (or divertimento) is still obvious in Johann Baptist Cramer's *Notturno* Op. 54 for piano (published c. 1816), where each of the two expressive movements is followed by one much more animated.

The Irish composer John Field deserves credit as the father of the Romantic nocturne. The musical narrative in his nocturnes unfolds without excessive drama or agogic contrast. The first, in E♭ major, and the fifth, in B♭ major, can be considered archetypal of the genre. The fourth in A major was Franz Liszt's favourite. In the final part of the Nocturne in E major, titled 'Midi', the twelve accented repetitions of the main note, reminiscent of the sound of a bell, transport the listener into a soft, dreamy mood. Its distant echo seems to be reflected in the lower register at the end of Chopin's Prelude in A♭ major, Op. 28 No. 17. As Carl Mikuli reports, Field's nocturnes were among Chopin's favourite works: not only did he play them with 'most charming ornaments', but he also included them in the repertoire he gave his pupils to study.[1]

Chopin composed twenty nocturnes, eighteen of them published during his lifetime. The first six were grouped in threes (Op. 9 and 15). Those in pairs are distinguished by their expressive and formal complementarity (Opp. 27, 32, 37, 48, 55 and 62). The Nocturne in E minor (Op. 72 No. 1) was published in 1855 by Julian Fontana as part of the *Œuvres posthumes de Chopin*; around 1870, the Baroness Nathaniel de Rothschild published the Nocturne in C minor under her own name.[2] An early composition of similar character – the *Lento con gran espressione* (published in 1875) – is often classified as a nocturne. In these quintessentially Romantic works, exploring many aspects of passion, the composer achieves perfection in the subtle deployment of lyrical and dramatic elements. They are considered the most beautiful of the genre and, in the Polish master's output, the purest incarnation of pianistic *bel canto*.

Among the large number of pieces bearing the title 'Nocturne' and written for the piano by Chopin's contemporaries, and then from 1850 onwards to the present day, a few stand out for their artistic quality: Maria Szymanowska's Nocturne in B♭ major, three *Notturnos* titled *Rêves d'amour* by Franz Liszt, and those by Alexander Scriabin, Gabriel Fauré, Sergei Rachmaninov, Louis Vierne and Francis Poulenc. At the age of thirty, Claude Debussy also composed a nocturne for piano in which Romantic lyricism blends wonderfully with impressionist harmonies.

Nineteenth-century piano literature also includes numerous pieces that do not bear this title, but are nevertheless close to the nocturne in their expressive, song-like quality. Robert Schumann's 'Des Abends' (*Fantasiestücke* Op. 12 No. 1) and Felix Mendelssohn-Bartholdy's 'Lied ohne Worte' Op. 62 No. 1 are eloquent examples, as are the slow movements of the two Chopin concertos. Chopin describes the mood of the Romance from his Op. 11 as follows:

> The *Adagio* [later changed to *Larghetto*] of the new concerto is in E major. It is not meant to be loud, it's more of a romance, quiet, melancholy; it should give the impression of gazing tenderly at a place which brings to the mind a thousand dear memories. It is a sort of meditation in beautiful spring weather, but by moonlight.[3]

Is this not a perfect description of the essence of a romantic nocturne?

Opus 9 is mentioned only occasionally in Chopin's correspondence. Thanks to Friederike Streicher-Müller, the first performance of the second nocturne can finally be identified more accurately: it was composed in Vienna, in the Artaria house at Kohlmarkt 9, where the composer stayed from November 1830 to July 1831.[4] We now know not only when and where this work was premiered, but also on what type of instrument: a 'marvellous' Graf piano.[5]

Together with the *Marche* (*funèbre*) from the Sonata Op. 35, Op. 9 No. 2 remains Chopin's best-known work. Financially, it was a very profitable investment for publishers of the time. The *Annotated Catalogue of Chopin's First Editions* (ACO) traces the rich and complex history of this short piece, of which the Leipzig publisher Kistner made no fewer than five successive engravings between 1833 and 1871.[6]

Form and design

In the case of 'a genre that does not fall into any of the established categories, in which feeling and melody reign alone, freed from the shackles and impediments of an obligatory form,'[7] it would be risky to seek a single, universal formal framework. However, a good many nocturnes from the Romantic period adopt a ternary ABA[1] construction, often followed by a coda. In Chopin's nocturnes, the middle section frequently introduces a change of character, becoming agitated (Op. 9 No. 3, Op. 15 No. 2, Op. 55 No. 1, Op. 62 No. 2), dramatic (Op. 15 No. 1, Op. 27 No. 1), religious/consolatory (Op. 15 No. 3, Op. 37 No. 1, Op. 48 No. 2) or dance-like (Op. 37 No. 2). Op. 15 No. 3 and the Nocturne in C minor adopt a more or less complex binary form in which the central part predominates because of its greater dimensions. Sometimes, in the ternary-form works, a concise version of the main theme reappears in an extended coda (for example, in Op. 55 No. 1). The form of the Nocturne Op. 27 No. 2 is rondo-like; that of Op. 9 No. 2 is a highly condensed, varied strophic form (characteristic of the lied and the romance), where the young Chopin brilliantly displays his talent over barely 34 bars.[8] The structure of this work is surprisingly ingenious: A, A[1], B, A[2], B[1], A[3], C, C[1]; each of these elements is based on foursquare phrases, and the last culminates in a cadenza leading to an even more concise ending, limited to two bars.

In conclusion, even if on the formal level some nocturnes present similarities, each one is unique. Any attempt to fit the music into a precise framework should be resisted: the form is entirely subject to inspiration and emotional impulses.

Performing the Nocturne Op. 9 No. 2

Nocturnes are lyrical, elegiac pieces that were very popular in the salons, and Chopin often included them in the programmes of his rare concerts. They were also part of the repertoire he gave his pupils to study. The Dubois, Stirling, Jędrzejewicz and Zaleska-Rosengardt copies contain numerous annotations, corrections and variants, while others have been handed down to us by tradition. In addition, Georges Mathias, Thomas D. A. Tellefsen and Carl Mikuli each left an edition of the master's works.[9]

---

[1] See pp. III and IV of the Preface to the complete edition of Chopin's works (Leipzig: Kistner, 1879). The volume with the nocturnes is available online at https://polona.pl/item/notturnos,ODI0ODE2MjQ/8/#info:metadata.

[2] On the attribution of this nocturne, see Jean-Jacques Eigeldinger, *Chopin et la baronne Nathaniel de Rothschild*, pp. 37–40.

[3] See letter of 15 May 1830 to Tytus Woyciechowski, *Chopin's Letters*, collected by Henryk Opieński, translated from the original Polish and French with a preface and editorial notes by E. L. Voynich (New York: Dover Publications, 1988), pp. 88–89.

[4] Uta Goebl-Streicher, 'Frédéric Chopin – Einblick in Unterricht und Umfeld. Die Briefe seiner Lieblingsschülerin Friederike Müller, Paris 1839–1845', in *Musikwissenschaftliche Schriften*, 51 (Munich-Salzburg: Katzbichler, 2018), letter no. 198, pp. 503–505.

[5] In his letter to his family of 22 December 1830, Chopin mentions this piano, describing it as 'cudny [marvelous]', *Korespondencja Fryderyka Chopina* (Warsaw: WUW, 2009), vol. I, pp. 453–455. The word was misread by Sydow as 'nudny [dull]'. See *Chopin's Letters*, p. 129.

[6] See https://chopinonline.ac.uk/aco/catalogue/nocturnes-opus-9.

[7] Liszt's definition. See the preface (titled 'Illustrations') to Field's *Nocturnes* (Leipzig: Schuberth & Co.), p. 4. Several versions of this volume were published successively in 1850, 1859, 1863, 1869 and 1876, respectively containing 6, 8, 9, 12 and 18 pieces.

[8] According to Lenz, who frequently played this piece for Chopin, 'the Nocturne is simply a perfected Field, grafted on a more interesting bass', and, according to him, Chopin shared this opinion. See Wilhelm von Lenz, *The Great Piano Virtuosos of Our Time from Personal Acquaintance*, p. 60.

[9] *Œuvres choisies pour piano par F. Chopin, édition revue et corrigée par G. Mathias* (Paris: Maison Lemoine aîné, Harand successeur, 1859), *Collection des œuvres pour le piano par Frédéric Chopin, en douze livraisons, publiée par T. D. A. Tellefsen* (Paris: Richault, 1860), *Fr. Chopin's Pianoforte-Werke, revid. u. m. Fingersatz versehen (zum grössten Theil nach des Autors Notirungen) v. Carl Mikuli* (Leipzig: Kistner, 1879–80).

The original version of Op. 9 No. 2, in its relative simplicity, stands in stark contrast to the version that reproduces all the variants known to date for this nocturne (see pp. 6–10 of this edition). The latter requires a special approach because of the abundance of embellishments and fioriture, as well as the increased technical difficulties; despite the tendency towards virtuosity, they must not in any way affect the intimate, singing character so well captured by the original version. In her letter cited in note 4, Friederike Streicher-Müller states that during her lesson on Thursday 13 May 1841 Chopin showed her all the ornamental variants, so that she could play this work exactly as he did. Did the original version – too reminiscent of Field (see note 7) and accessible to less experienced pianists – no longer satisfy the composer's refined taste? Only he could have answered this question.

Even if they seem obvious today, the following remarks by Chopin's pupils may be useful. Mikuli observes that in working on the nocturnes 'the pupil should learn to recognize, love and perform the beautiful, smooth sound of singing'.[10] When Wilhelm von Lenz was working on Op. 9 No. 2, the composer advised him to study the left-hand part separately (initially dividing it between two hands) in order to achieve absolute regularity in the accompaniment, over which a full-throated song can then unfold with complete freedom, its expression intensifying in each successive variation of the theme. According to Adolf Gutmann's testimony, reported by Frederick Niecks, Chopin played the undulating accompaniment in many of these pieces 'very soft and subdued'.[11] The talented pianist Friederike Streicher-Müller also emphasized the importance of a regular and independent left hand.[12] Lacking sufficient dynamic indications in the first editions, she had to repeat the second nocturne in Op. 37 seven times before fully satisfying her demanding teacher.[13]

These works raise the thorny problem of metronomic indications. From Op. 28 onwards, these are no longer specified either in Chopin's manuscripts or in the editions. On the other hand, those provided for the first eight nocturnes are surprisingly fast. As for Op. 9 No. 2, the reference value given in the first editions is simply wrong ('♩' or '♩.' instead of '♪'; see also the discussion in the Critical Commentary). Pianists have long been playing not only this work but also most of Chopin's nocturnes at more moderate tempos, which they feel are better suited both to the Romantic lyricism and to fuller-sounding modern instruments.

Raoul Pugno, who studied at the Paris Conservatoire with one of Chopin's few professional pupils, Georges Mathias, drew attention to a practice that was widespread in the past and persists today, giving this sound advice: 'Over and over again I practise playing the two hands very much together. To hear in every bar the bass preceding the note of the right hand is truly exasperating and anti-musical.'[14] This is food for thought and, above all, a recommendation to be applied.

Another important question should also be raised: is it possible to perform Chopin's nocturnes, which contain such a multitude of ornaments and fioriture, without any flexibility according to a rule that requires the left hand to maintain the movement strictly (acting as a Kapellmeister, a clock) while leaving the right free to break away from the metric constraints? In our opinion, the best answer, closely related to the understanding of *tempo rubato*,[15] is Raoul Koczalski's, even if it seems to contradict that of his teacher Carl Mikuli (summarized above):

> The famous *tempo rubato*, which was so debated, is nothing more than a rapid, abrupt change of tempo. If the right hand plays the melody quietly, slowly or quickly, the left hand should be equally slow or fast and follow the right hand. The musical phrase should be divided in such a way that for each note or chord struck by the left hand there is a number of equal notes in the right hand, so that both hands can always play at the same time. Only in a few passages, for example when the right hand is performing grace notes or when, driven by the warmth of the feeling it expresses, whether hesitant or determined, it seeks to free itself from the left hand, only then can there be a barely noticeable difference between the touch of the two hands. But such cases are extremely rare and must be treated with utmost care.[16]

The literature on Chopin is vast. His life, work, teaching, virtuosity and inimitable approach to the piano are constantly the subject of scientific publications that expand our knowledge. However, to fully appreciate his genius, one would have loved to attend Emilie von Gretsch's lesson, during which she had the privilege of hearing her teacher perform his nocturnes twice, or to be in the shoes of Charles Hallé, who, after hearing Chopin play, wrote: 'That was beyond all words. The few senses I had quite left me. I could have jumped into the Seine. … I can confidently assert that nobody has ever been able to reproduce [his works] as they sounded under his magical fingers.'[17]

Further reading

Eigeldinger, Jean-Jacques, *Chopin et la baronne Nathaniel de Rothschild, Nocturne en ut mineur et Valse en la mineur sans numéro d'opus, problèmes d'attribution* (Warsaw: NIFC, 2016).

— *Chopin vu par ses élèves* (Paris: Fayard, 2006). In English: *Chopin: Pianist and Teacher as Seen by his Pupils*, trans. Naomi Shohet, Krysia Osostowicz and Roy Howat, ed. Roy Howat (Cambridge: Cambridge University Press, 1986).

Koczalski, Raoul, *Frédéric Chopin, Conseils d'interprétation, Introduction par Jean-Jacques Eigeldinger* (Paris: Buchet/Chastel, 1998).

Lenz, Wilhelm von, *The Great Piano Virtuosos of Our Time from Personal Acquaintance: Liszt, Chopin, Tausig, Henselt,* translated from the German by Madeleine R. Baker (New York: Schirmer, 1899; reprint New York: Da Capo Press, 1973).

Pugno, Raoul, *Les Leçons écrites de Raoul Pugno, Chopin* (Paris: Librairie des Annales, 1909).

Rink, John, '"Structural Momentum" and Closure in Chopin's Nocturne Op. 9, No. 2', in *Schenker Studies 2*, ed. Carl Schachter and Hedi Siegel (Cambridge: Cambridge University Press, 1999), pp. 109–126.

Christophe Grabowski
(Translation: Dennis Collins)

I would particularly like to thank Jean-Jacques Eigeldinger and John Rink for their valuable advice in the preparation of this edition.

---

[10] See p. IV of the preface cited in note 1.

[11] Frederick Niecks, *Frederick Chopin as a Man and Musician* (London & New York: Novello, Ewer Co., 1888), vol. II, p. 264, note 33 (available at https://polona.pl/item/frederick-chopin-as-a-man-and-musician-in-two-volumes-vol-2,MTE4NzEzMA/138/#item).

[12] Uta Goebl-Streicher, 'Frédéric Chopin', letters nos. 70 and 71, pp. 121 and 124. She specifically mentions the Nocturnes Op. 27, but her remarks apply as well to Op. 9 No. 2.

[13] Ibid., letter no. 119, p. 272. The manuscripts of this work that Chopin delivered to his publishers included very few dynamics. He added some to Dubois' copy.

[14] Raoul Pugno, *Les Leçons écrites de Raoul Pugno, Chopin*, p. 66. Pugno thus follows in the footsteps of Thalberg, who also denounced this practice, condemning 'the striking of melodic notes long after the accompaniment'. However, Thalberg qualifies his position and finds that 'in a slow melody written in long values, a nice effect, especially on the first beat of each bar or at the beginning of each section of the melody, is to play the singing part after the bass, but only with an almost imperceptible delay'. See Sigismund Thalberg, *L'Art du chant appliqué au piano / Die Kunst des Gesanges auf dem Pianoforte* (Leipzig: Breitkopf & Härtel, 1853), p. 2 (available at https://polona.pl/item/choeur-des-conjures-de-l-opera-il-crociato-de-meyerbeer-op-70,MTA0MTY1MTQy/3/#info:metadata). In their Chopin recordings, Pugno and Koczalski frequently play the right hand slightly after the left, in accordance with Thalberg's advice. Yet, like Pugno, Koczalski also claimed that 'both hands should strike at the same time and with great precision'; see Raoul Koczalski, *Frédéric Chopin, Conseils d'interprétation*, p. 62.

[15] This indication, which appears in Chopin's music mostly in folk-inspired contexts, is used only twice in the nocturnes: in Op. 9 No. 2 (bar 26) and in Op. 15 No. 3 (bar 1). It is noteworthy that in Stirling's copy of the latter work the words *languido* and *rubato* have been struck out.

[16] Raoul Koczalski, *Frédéric Chopin, Conseils d'interprétation*, pp. 62–63.

[17] Jean-Jacques Eigeldinger, *Chopin: Pianist and Teacher,* pp. 79–80, 271.

PRÉFACE

Genre et genèse

Le soir, le crépuscule et la nuit furent et demeurent toujours des sources d'inspiration pour de nombreux poètes, peintres et musiciens. Dans le domaine de la musique, c'est incontestablement le nocturne dans sa version pour piano qui se hisse au sommet du palmarès des genres évocateurs de la nuit. Avant de devenir l'une des manifestations les plus emblématiques du lyrisme romantique et l'expression pure du *bel canto*, ce titre était déjà utilisé pour des pièces comprenant plusieurs mouvements de caractère diversifié, composées pour un petit ensemble instrumental et destinées à agrémenter une fête nocturne. A titre d'exemples, citons les huit *Notturni* Hob. II:25-32 composés pour le roi Ferdinand IV de Naples de Joseph Haydn, puis la *Serenata notturna* K. 239 et le *Notturno* K. 286 de Wolfgang Amadeus Mozart. L'influence de la sérénade (ou du *divertimento*) est encore bien présente dans le *Notturno* op. 54 pour piano de Johann Baptist Cramer (paru c. 1816) où chacune des deux parties expressives est suivie d'une d'un caractère nettement plus animé.

Le privilège de la paternité du nocturne romantique revient au compositeur irlandais John Field. Dans ses nocturnes, aucune véritable tempête ne vient perturber une narration musicale dénuée du dramatisme, se déroulant sans grands contrastes agogiques. Le premier en *Mi* majeur et le cinquième en *Si* majeur peuvent être considérés comme archétypes du genre. Le quatrième en *La* majeur était le préféré de Franz Liszt. Dans la partie finale du Nocturne en *Mi* majeur appelé « Midi », les 12 répétitions accentuées de la note principale, évoquant le son d'une cloche, transportent l'auditeur dans une ambiance douce et rêveuse. On dirait que son écho lointain se réfléchit dans un registre grave à la fin du Prélude en *Lab* majeur op. 28 n°17 de Chopin. Comme le rapporte Carl Mikuli, les nocturnes de Field faisaient partie des œuvres de prédilection du compositeur polonais ; non seulement il les jouait en y improvisant « des fioritures du plus grand charme », mais les incluait également dans le répertoire à étudier par ses élèves[1].

Chopin composa vingt nocturnes dont dix-huit furent publiés de son vivant. Les six premiers furent groupés par trois (op. 9 et 15). Ceux réunis en « couple » se distinguent par une complémentarité expressive et formelle (op. 27, 32, 37, 48, 55 et 62). Le Nocturne en *mi* mineur (op. 72 n° 1) fut édité en 1855 par Julian Fontana, dans le cadre des *Œuvres posthumes de Chopin* ; c. 1870, la baronne Nathaniel de Rothschild publia sous son propre nom celui en *ut* mineur[2]. Une composition de jeunesse de caractère similaire – le *Lento con gran espressione* (paru en 1875) – est souvent classée comme nocturne. Dans ces œuvres d'essence romantique, explorant de nombreux aspects de la passion, le compositeur réussit à atteindre la perfection dans le déploiement subtil des éléments lyriques et dramatiques. Elles sont considérées comme les plus belles du genre et, dans la production du maître polonais, comme la plus pure incarnation du *bel canto* pianistique.

Dans l'impressionnante quantité de pièces portant ce titre, écrites pour piano par les contemporains de Chopin, puis, à partir 1850 et jusqu'à nos jours, remarquons-en, sans être exhaustifs, quelques-unes qui se distinguent par leur qualité artistique : le Nocturne en *Si* majeur de Maria Szymanowska, trois *Notturnos* intitulés *Rêves d'amour* de Franz Liszt, ceux d'Alexandre Scriabine, Gabriel Fauré, Sergueï Rachmaninov, Louis Vierne et de Francis Poulenc. A l'âge de 30 ans, Claude Debussy composa un nocturne pour piano dans lequel le lyrisme encore romantique se marie à merveille avec des harmonies déjà impressionnistes.

La littérature pour piano du XIXᵉ siècle est également riche en pièces qui ne portent pas ce titre, mais tout en étant proches du nocturne par leur côté expressif et chantant. « Des Abends » (*Fantasiestücke* op. 12 n° 1) de Robert Schumann et « Lied ohne Worte » op. 62 n° 1 de Felix Mendelssohn-Bartholdy en sont des exemples éloquents, comme également les mouvements lents des deux concertos de Chopin. L'ambiance de la *Romance* de l'Opus 11 est décrite ainsi par le compositeur :

L'*Adagio* [modifié plus tard en *Larghetto*] du nouveau *Concerto* est en *Mi* majeur. Je n'y ai pas recherché la force. C'est plutôt une romance calme et mélancolique qui doit faire l'impression d'un doux regard tourné vers un lieu évoquant mille charmants souvenirs. C'est comme une rêverie par un beau temps printanier, mais au clair de lune[3].

N'est-ce pas une parfaite description de l'essence même d'un nocturne romantique ?

L'Opus 9 n'est mentionné qu'épisodiquement dans la correspondance de Chopin. Grâce à Friederike Streicher-Müller, la création du second nocturne peut enfin être cernée avec plus d'exactitude : il fut composé à Vienne, dans la maison Artaria [Kohlmarkt 9] où le compositeur séjourna de novembre 1830 à juillet 1831[4]. A présent, nous savons non seulement quand et où cette œuvre a été créée, mais également sur quelle marque d'instruments : un « magnifique » piano Graf[5].

Avec la *Marche* (*funèbre*) de la *Sonate* op. 35, l'Opus 9 n° 2 demeure l'œuvre la plus connue du compositeur polonais. Commercialement parlant, il fut un investissement très rentable pour les éditeurs de l'époque. L'*Annotated Catalogue of Chopin's First Editions* (*ACO*) retrace l'histoire riche et complexe de cette courte pièce dont l'éditeur leipzigois Kistner réalisa cinq gravures successives entre 1833 et 1871[6].

Forme et conception

Dans le cas « d'un genre ne relevant d'aucune des catégories établies, dans lequel le sentiment et la mélodie règnent seuls, délivrés des entraves et des alourdissements d'une forme obligée »[7], il serait périlleux de chercher un cadre formel unique et universel. Cependant, bon nombre de nocturnes de l'époque romantique épousent une construction ternaire ABA[1] suivie souvent d'une coda. Dans ceux de Chopin, la partie centrale apporte fréquemment un changement de caractère qui devient agité (op. 9 n° 3, op. 15 n° 2, op. 55 n° 1, op. 62 n° 2), dramatique (op. 15 n° 1, op. 27 n° 1), religieux/apaisant (op. 15 n° 3, op. 37 n° 1, op. 48 n° 2) ou dansant (op. 37 n° 2). Le Nocturne op. 15 n° 3 et celui en *ut* mineur épousent une forme binaire plus ou moins complexe dans laquelle la partie centrale prédomine par ses dimensions plus développées. Parfois, dans ceux d'une forme ternaire, le thème principal réapparaît dans une version lapidaire au profit d'une coda élargie (par exemple, dans l'op. 55 n° 1). La forme du Nocturne op. 27 n° 2 est proche du rondo ; celle – très condensée – de l'Opus 9 n° 2 d'une forme strophique variée (caractéristique du *Lied* et de la romance) où en 34 mesures à peine le talent du juvénile Chopin se manifeste dans tout son éclat[8]. La structure de cette œuvre surprend par son ingéniosité : A, A¹, B, A², B¹, A³, C, C¹ – chacun de ces éléments est tributaire de la carrure ; le dernier, se termine par une *cadenza* aboutissant sur une conclusion encore plus concise, limitée à deux mesures.

En conclusion, même si sur le plan formel certains nocturnes présentent des similitudes, chacun d'eux est unique. Dans leur cas, la préoccupation de faire rentrer la musique dans un cadre précis est secondaire. La forme y est entièrement soumise à l'inspiration et aux élans émotionnels.

---

[1] Voir les p. III et IV de la Préface à l'édition complète des œuvres de Chopin (Leipzig, Kistner, 1879). Le volume des Nocturnes est disponible en ligne à : https://polona.pl/item/notturnos,ODI0ODE2MjQ/8/#info:metadata

[2] Au sujet de l'attribution de ce nocturne voir : Jean-Jacques Eigeldinger, *Chopin et la baronne Nathaniel de Rothschild* [...], p. 37-40.

[3] Voir la lettre du 15 mai 1830 adressée à Tytus Woyciechowski, *Correspondance de Frédéric Chopin* [...] (Paris, Richard Masse, 1981), vol. I, p. 166.

[4] Uta Goebl-Streicher, « Frédéric Chopin - Einblick in Unterricht und Umfeld. Die Briefe seiner Lieblingsschülerin Friederike Müller, Paris 1839-1845 », in *Musikwissenschaftliche Schriften*, 51 (Munich-Salzburg, Katzbichler, 2018), lettre n° 198, p. 503-505.

[5] Dans la lettre à sa famille du 22 décembre 1830, Chopin fait mention de ce piano en le qualifiant de « cudny » [magnifique, merveilleux], *Korespondencja Fryderyka Chopina* (Warszawa, WUW, 2009), vol. I, p. 453-455. Ce qualificatif a été déformé par Sydow en « ennuyeux » [nudny]. Voir : *Correspondance de Frédéric Chopin* [...], *op. cit.*, vol. I, p. 235.

[6] Voir : https://chopinonline.ac.uk/aco/catalogue/nocturnes-opus-9.

[7] Définition venant de Liszt, voir la Préface (intitulée « Illustrations ») aux *Nocturnes* de Field (Leipzig, Schuberth & Co.), p. 4. Il existe plusieurs versions de ce volume, sorties successivement en 1850, 1859, 1863, 1869 et 1876, contenant 6, 8, 9, 12 et 18 pièces.

[8] D'après von Lenz qui rabâchait les oreilles de Chopin avec cette pièce, « elle n'est rien d'autre qu'une greffe de Field entée sur des basses plus intéressantes » et, d'après ses dires, le compositeur partageait cette opinion. Voir : Wilhelm von Lenz, *Les Grands Virtuoses du Piano, Liszt - Chopin - Tausig - Henselt*, p. 80.

Interprétation du Nocturne op. 9 n° 2

Le nocturne étant l'élément lyrique, élégiaque apprécié dans les salons, Chopin incluait souvent ces pièces dans le programme de ses rares concerts. De même, elles faisaient partie du répertoire à étudier par ses élèves. Les exemplaires Dubois, Stirling, Jędrzejewicz, Zaleska-Rosengardt enferment de nombreuses annotations, corrections et variantes, d'autres nous ont été transmises par la tradition. Par ailleurs, Georges Mathias, Thomas D. A. Tellefsen et Carl Mikuli ont laissé chacun son édition de l'œuvre du maître[9].

Par sa relative simplicité, la version originale de l'op. 9 n° 2 marque un net contraste avec celle qui reproduit toutes les variantes connues à ce jour pour ce nocturne (voir les pages 6-10 de la présente publication). Cette dernière demande une approche particulière du fait de l'abondance des fioritures et arabesques, ainsi qu'un niveau pianistique en rapport avec l'accroissement des difficultés techniques ; celles-ci, poussant vers la virtuosité, ne doivent aucunement influer sur le caractère intime et chantant si bien rendu par la version originale. Dans sa lettre citée dans la note 4, Friederike Streicher-Müller précise qu'au cours de sa leçon du jeudi 13 mai 1841, le maître lui montra toutes les variantes ornementales, afin qu'elle puisse jouer cette œuvre exactement comme lui. La version originale faisant trop penser à Field (voir la note 7), accessible aux pianistes moins chevronnés, ne satisfaisait-elle plus le goût raffiné de son créateur ? A cette question lui seul le connaissait la réponse.

Même si aujourd'hui elles paraissent évidentes, les remarques qui suivent, émanant des élèves de Chopin, peuvent nous être utiles. Mikuli observe qu'en travaillant les nocturnes « l'élève devrait se familiariser avec le *legato*, apprendre à aimer et à reproduire le beau son lié du chant »[10]. Lors de l'apprentissage de l'Opus 9 n° 2, le compositeur conseilla à Wilhelm von Lenz d'étudier séparément la partie de la main gauche (en la répartissant, dans un premier temps, entre deux mains) afin de parvenir à une régularité absolue de l'accompagnement sur lequel peut ensuite se déployer en toute liberté un large chant dont l'expression s'intensifie dans chacune des variantes successives du thème. D'après le témoignage d'Adolf Gutmann rapporté par Frederick Niecks, Chopin faisait jouer très doux et à mi-voix l'accompagnement en mouvement ondulatoire présent dans bon nombre de ces pièces[11]. La talentueuse pianiste Friederike Streicher-Müller souligne également l'importance de la régularité et l'indépendance de la main gauche[12]. Faute d'indications dynamiques suffisantes dans les premières éditions, elle a dû répéter 7 fois le second nocturne de l'Opus 37 avant de satisfaire pleinement son exigeant professeur[13].

Un épineux problème, celui des indications métronomiques, se pose pour ces œuvres. A partir de l'Opus 28, elles ne sont plus précisées ni dans les manuscrits ni dans les éditions. Mais, celles indiquées pour les huit premiers nocturnes surprennent par leur rapidité. Quant à l'Opus 9 n° 2, la valeur de référence indiquée dans les premières éditions est tout simplement fausse (« ♩ » ou « ♩. » à la place de « ♪ » ; voir aussi la discussion dans le Commentaire critique). Depuis longtemps, les pianistes jouent non seulement cette œuvre, mais également la plupart des nocturnes de Chopin dans des tempos plus modérés qui, à leurs yeux, sont mieux adaptés aussi bien au lyrisme romantique qu'aux instruments modernes pourvus d'une sonorité plus ample.

Raoul Pugno ayant travaillé au Conservatoire de Paris avec Georges Mathias – l'un des rares élèves professionnels de Chopin – attire l'attention sur une pratique très répandue autrefois et persistante encore de nos jours, en donnant ce conseil judicieux : « je répéterai sans cesse de jouer les deux mains très ensemble. Entendre dans chaque mesure la basse précéder la note de la main droite est vraiment une chose horripilante et anti-musicale »[14]. Voilà une matière à réflexion et surtout une recommandation à appliquer.

Une question importante est également à soulever : est-il possible d'interpréter sans souplesse les nocturnes de Chopin enfermant une telle multitude d'ornements et d'arabesques et d'y appliquer la règle qui impose à la main gauche de maintenir rigoureusement le mouvement (être le maître de chapelle, une horloge) tout en laissant à la main droite la liberté de s'affranchir du carcan métrique ? A notre avis, la meilleure réponse, liée étroitement à la compréhension du tempo *rubato*[15], provient de Raoul Koczalski, même si elle semble être en contradiction avec celle de son professeur Carl Mikuli (résumée juste avant) :

> Le fameux tempo *rubato*, qui fut tant disputé, n'est autre chose qu'un rapide et brusque changement de mouvement. Si la main droite joue la mélodie d'une façon discrète, lente ou bien rapide, la main gauche doit avoir la même lenteur ou la même rapidité et suivre la main droite. Il faut partager la phrase musicale de telle sorte qu'à chaque note ou à chaque accord frappé par la main gauche correspondent un certain nombre de notes égales à la main droite, afin que les deux mains puissent toujours jouer en même temps. Dans quelques passages seulement, par exemple lorsque la main droite exécute des notes d'agrément ou quand, entraînée par la chaleur du sentiment qu'elle exprime, hésitante ou résolue, elle cherche à se libérer de la main gauche, alors seulement il peut y avoir une différence à peine sensible entre le toucher des deux mains. Mais de telles cas sont extrêmement rares et doivent être traités avec la plus grande précaution[16].

La littérature consacrée à Chopin est très abondante. Sa vie, son œuvre, son enseignement, sa virtuosité et son approche inimitable du piano font constamment l'objet de publications scientifiques qui élargissent nos connaissances. Cependant, pour pouvoir apprécier pleinement son génie, on aurait tant aimé assister à la leçon d'Emilie von Gretsch au cours de laquelle elle eut le privilège d'entendre son maître interpréter à deux reprises ses nocturnes ou être à la place de Charles Hallé qui, après avoir entendu Chopin jouer, écrivit « Ce fut au-delà de toute parole. Le peu de bon sens qui me restait m'a complètement abandonné. J'aurais pu me jeter dans la Seine. […] Je puis affirmer en conscience que personne n'a jamais été à même d'exécuter ses œuvres telles qu'elles sonnaient sous ses doigts magiques »[17].

Bibliographie selective

Eigeldinger, Jean-Jacques, *Chopin et la baronne Nathaniel de Rothschild, Nocturne en ut mineur et Valse en la mineur sans numéro d'opus, problèmes d'attribution* (Varsovie, NIFC, 2016).
— *Chopin vu par ses élèves* (Paris, Fayard, 2006).
Koczalski, Raoul, *Frédéric Chopin, Conseils d'interprétation, Introduction par Jean-Jacques Eigeldinger* (Paris, Buchet/Chastel, 1998).
Lenz, Wilhelm von, *Les Grands Virtuoses du Piano, Liszt - Chopin - Tausig - Henselt, traduit et présenté par Jean-Jacques Eigeldinger* (Paris, Flammarion, 1995).
Pugno, Raoul, *Les Leçons écrites de Raoul Pugno, Chopin* (Paris, Librairie des Annales, 1909).
Rink, John, « 'Structural Momentum' and Closure in Chopin's Nocturne Op. 9, No. 2 », in *Schenker Studies 2*, éd. Carl Schachter et Hedi Siegel (Cambridge, Cambridge University Press, 1999), p. 109-126.

Christophe Grabowski

Je tiens à remercier plus particulièrement Jean-Jacques Eigeldinger et John Rink pour leurs précieux conseils lors de la préparation de cette édition.

---

[9] *Œuvres choisies pour piano par F. Chopin, édition revue et corrigée par G. Mathias* (Paris, Maison Lemoine aîné, Harand successeur, 1859), *Collection des œuvres pour le piano par Frédéric Chopin, en douze livraisons, publiée par T. D. A. Tellefsen* (Paris, Richault 1860), *Fr. Chopin's Pianoforte-Werke, revid. u. m. Fingersatz versehen (zum grössten Theil nach des Autors Notirungen) v. Carl Mikuli* (Leipzig, Kistner, 1879-1880).

[10] Voir la p. IV de la Préface citée dans la note 1.

[11] Frederick Niecks, *Frederick Chopin as a Man and Musician* (London & New York, Novello, Ewer Co., 1888), vol. II, p. 264, note 33 (consultable à https://polona.pl/item/frederick-chopin-as-a-man-and-musician-in-two-volumes-vol-2,MTE4NzEzMA/138/#item).

[12] Uta Goebl-Streicher, « Frédéric Chopin », *op. cit.*, lettres n° 70 et 71, p. 121 et 124. Il y est question des Nocturnes op. 27, mais les propos s'appliquent aussi bien à l'Opus 9 n° 2.

[13] *Ibid.*, lettre n° 119, p. 272. Les manuscrits de cette œuvre délivrés par Chopin à ses éditeurs comportaient très peu de nuances. Il en indiqua quelques-unes dans l'exemplaire Dubois.

[14] Raoul Pugno, *Les Leçons écrites de Raoul Pugno, Chopin*, p. 66. Pugno se place ainsi dans la continuité de Thalberg qui, lui-aussi, dénonça cette pratique en condamnant « le frappement des notes de chant longtemps après celles de la basse ». Cependant, Thalberg nuance sa position et trouve que « dans une mélodie lente écrite en notes de longue durée, il est d'un bon effet, surtout au premier temps de chaque mesure ou en commençant chaque période de phrase, d'attaquer le chant après la basse, mais seulement avec un retard presque imperceptible. », voir : Sigismund Thalberg, *L'art du chant appliqué au piano* (Leipzig, Breitkopf & Härtel, 1853), p. 2 (consultable à https://polona.pl/item/choeur-des-conjures-de-l-opera-il-crociato-de-meyerbeer-op-70,MTA0MTY1MTQy/3/#info:metadata). Dans leurs enregistrements chopéniens, Pugno et Koczalski décalent fréquemment d'une façon serrée la main gauche par rapport à la droite, suivant ce que préconise Thalberg. Pourtant, comme Pugno, Koczalski affirma aussi que « les deux mains doivent frapper en même temps et avec une grande précision », voir : Raoul Koczalski, *Frédéric Chopin, Conseils d'interprétation*, p. 62.

[15] Cette indication qui par ailleurs figure essentiellement dans des contextes folklorisants n'apparaît que deux fois dans les nocturnes : dans l'op. 9 n° 2 (mes. 26) et dans l'op. 15 n° 3 (mes. 1). Notons que dans l'exemplaire Stirling de la seconde œuvre mentionnée le *languido* accompagné du *rubato* ont été barrés.

[16] Raoul Koczalski, *Frédéric Chopin, Conseils d'interprétation*, p. 62-63.

[17] Jean-Jacques Eigeldinger, *Chopin vu par ses élèves*, p. 111, 343-344.

VORWORT

Gattung und Entstehung

Der Abend, die Dämmerung und die Nacht inspirieren von jeher und bis heute zahlreiche Dichter, Maler und Musiker. In der Musik ist das Nocturne für Klavier der unbestrittene Gipfelpunkt der Gattungen, die die Nacht heraufbeschwören. Doch schon bevor diese Stückbezeichnung zu einer der prägnantesten Erscheinungsformen des romantischen Lyrismus wurde, zum reinen Ausdruck des *Belcanto*, findet sie sich als Titel, beispielsweise bei Joseph Haydn: acht *Notturni* Hob. II:25–32, komponiert für Ferdinand IV., König von Neapel, und bei Wolfgang Amadeus Mozart: *Serenata notturna* KV 239 und *Notturno* KV 286. Diese Stücke enthalten mehrere Sätze unterschiedlichen Charakters, sind für eine kleine Instrumentalbesetzung geschrieben und waren zur musikalischen Untermalung nächtlicher Festlichkeiten bestimmt. Noch deutlich spürbar ist der Einfluss der Serenade (oder des Divertimento) im *Notturno* op. 54 für Klavier von Johann Baptist Cramer (erschienen um 1816), in dem auf jeden der beiden ausdrucksvollen Abschnitte ein deutlich lebhafterer folgt.

Die Schöpfung des romantischen Nocturnes ist das Verdienst des irischen Komponisten John Field. In seinen Nocturnes wird die musikalische Erzählung nie von echten stürmischen Wallungen erregt und kommt ohne größere agogische Kontraste aus. Das erste Nocturne in Es-Dur und das fünfte in B-Dur können als Archetypen des Genres angesehen werden. Franz Liszt bevorzugte das vierte, in A-Dur. Im letzten Teil des Nocturnes E-Dur mit dem Beinamen „Midi" („Mittag") versetzen die zwölf akzentuierten Schläge der Grundnote, die an den Klang einer Glocke erinnern, den Hörer in eine sanfte und träumerische Stimmung. Ihr fernes Echo scheint gegen Ende von Chopins As-Dur-Prélude op. 28 Nr. 17 im tiefen Register nachzuhallen. Carl Mikuli berichtet, dass Fields Nocturnes zu den Lieblingswerken des polnischen Komponisten gehörten; er spielte sie nicht nur, indem er dazu „die reizendsten Verzierungen" improvisierte, sondern nahm sie auch in das Repertoire auf, das er seine Schüler studieren ließ.[1]

Chopin komponierte 20 Nocturnes, von denen 18 zu seinen Lebzeiten veröffentlicht wurden. Dabei waren die ersten sechs in zwei Dreiergruppen zusammengefasst (op. 9 und 15). Die als Werkpaare veröffentlichten Nocturnes sind komplementär in Ausdruck und Form (op. 27, 32, 37, 48, 55 und 62). Das Nocturne e-Moll (op. 72 Nr. 1) wurde 1855 von Julian Fontana in den *Œuvres posthumes de Chopin* herausgegeben; um 1870 veröffentlichte die Baronin Charlotte de Rothschild das Nocturne in c-Moll unter ihrem eigenen Namen.[2] Ein Jugendwerk ähnlichen Charakters – das *Lento con gran espressione* (erschienen 1875) – wird häufig den Nocturnes zugerechnet. In diesen Werken romantischen Charakters gelangt der Komponist, indem er die Leidenschaft unter zahlreichen Aspekten erkundet, in der subtilen Entfaltung lyrischer und dramatischer Elemente zur Perfektion. Sie werden als die schönsten Vertreter der Gattung angesehen und im Schaffen des polnischen Komponisten als reinster Ausdruck des pianistischen *Belcanto*.

Von der beeindruckenden Vielzahl an Stücken unter diesem Titel, die von Chopins Zeitgenossen und später, ab 1850 und bis heute, für das Klavier geschrieben wurden, seien an dieser Stelle stellvertretend nur einige genannt, die sich durch ihre künstlerische Qualität auszeichnen: das Nocturne B-Dur von Maria Szymanowska, drei *Notturnos* mit dem Titel *Rêves d'amour* von Franz Liszt sowie die Nocturnes von Alexander Skrjabin, Gabriel Fauré, Sergej Rachmaninow, Louis Vierne und Francis Poulenc. Im Alter von 30 Jahren schrieb Claude Debussy ein Nocturne für Klavier, dessen noch romantischer Lyrismus nahtlos mit bereits impressionistischen Harmonien verschmilzt.

Die Klavierliteratur des 19. Jahrhunderts ist außerdem reich an Stücken, die, ohne diesen Titel zu tragen, dem Nocturne in ihrem Ausdruck und ihrer Sanglichkeit nahestehen. „Des Abends" (*Fantasiestücke* op. 12 Nr. 1) von Robert Schumann und das „Lied ohne Worte" op. 62 Nr. 1 von Felix Mendelssohn Bartholdy sind dafür genauso beredte Beispiele wie die langsamen Sätze aus den beiden Konzerten Chopins. Die Stimmung der *Romance* aus seinem Opus 11 beschreibt der Komponist folgendermaßen:

Das [später in *Larghetto* umbenannte] *Adagio* des neuen Konzerts ist in E-Dur. (Es soll nicht tüchtig sein.) Es ist mehr romantisch, ruhig und melancholisch; es soll den Eindruck eines liebevollen Hinblickens auf eine Stätte machen, die tausende von angenehmen Erinnerungen aufsteigen lässt. Es ist wie ein Hinträumen in einer mondbeglänzten Frühlingsnacht.[3]

Liest sich diese Stelle nicht wie eine perfekte Beschreibung der Wesenhaftigkeit eines romantischen Nocturnes?

Von Opus 9 ist in Chopins Briefen nur gelegentlich die Rede. Dank Friederike Streicher-Müller lässt sich die Entstehungszeit des zweiten Nocturnes endlich genauer eingrenzen: Es wurde in Wien im Artaria-Haus [Kohlmarkt 9] komponiert, wo der Komponist zwischen November 1830 und Juli 1831 seinen Aufenthalt hatte.[4] Wir wissen jetzt nicht nur, wann und wo dieses Werk geschaffen wurde, sondern kennen auch die Marke des dabei verwendeten Instruments: ein „herrliches" Klavier von Graf.[5]

Neben dem *Marche* (*funèbre*, dem „Trauermarsch") aus der *Sonate* op. 35 bleibt Opus 9 Nr. 2 das bekannteste Werk des polnischen Komponisten. Auch in kommerzieller Hinsicht erwies es sich für die zeitgenössischen Verleger als durchaus rentabel. Der *Annotated Catalogue of Chopin's First Editions* (*ACO*) erzählt die reiche und komplexe Geschichte dieses kurzen Stücks, das der Leipziger Verleger Kistner zwischen 1833 und 1871 fünfmal stechen ließ.[6]

Form und Gestaltung

Es wäre gewagt, bei einer Gattung, „die ihren Ursprung von keiner der bestehenden Formen herschrieb, in welcher die Empfindung und der Gesang ausschliesslich vorherrschten, frei von den Fesseln und Schlacken einer aufgedrungenen Form",[7] nach einer einzigen, allgemeingültigen formalen Anlage zu suchen. Dessen ungeachtet sind viele Nocturnes der Romantik in einer dreiteiligen ABA-Form gehalten, der häufig eine Coda folgt. In Chopins Nocturnes wechselt die Stimmung häufig im Mittelteil und nimmt einen rastlosen (op. 9 Nr. 3, op. 15 Nr. 2, op. 55 Nr. 1, op. 62 Nr. 2), dramatischen (op. 15 Nr. 1, op. 27 Nr. 1), religiösen/ruhevollen (op. 15 Nr. 3, op. 37 Nr. 1, op. 48 Nr. 2) oder tänzerischen (op. 37 Nr. 2) Charakter an. Das Nocturne op. 15 Nr. 3 und das in c-Moll haben eine mehr oder minder komplexe zweiteilige Form, wobei der Kopfteil durch seinen ausgedehnteren Umfang gewichtiger ist. In der dreiteiligen Form kehrt das Hauptthema manchmal verknappt wieder, um einer erweiterten Coda Raum zu geben (z. B. in op. 55 Nr. 1). Das Nocturne op. 27 Nr. 2 nähert sich der Rondoform an, op. Nr. 2 einer – äußerst komprimierten – variierten Strophenform (wie sie für das Lied und die Romanze typisch ist). In gerade einmal 34 Takten offenbart sich hier zur Gänze das Talent des jungen Chopin.[8] Die Struktur des Werks überrascht durch ihren Einfallsreichtum: A, A¹, B, A², B¹, A³, C, C¹ – jedes dieser Elemente ist vierteilig. Das letzte endet in einer Kadenz mit einem noch knapperen Abschluss, der sich auf zwei Takte beschränkt.

Zusammenfassend lässt sich sagen, dass, auch wenn einige Nocturnes formale Gemeinsamkeiten aufweisen, doch jedes einzigartig bleibt. Das Anliegen, die Musik in einen festen Rahmen zu zwängen, wird hier nebensächlich. Die Form ergibt sich in den Nocturnes ganz aus der Eingebung und den Regungen der Gefühle.

---

[1] Vgl. S. III und IV des Vorworts zur Chopin-Gesamtausgabe (Leipzig, Kistner, 1879). Der Band mit den Nocturnes ist online zugänglich: https://polona.pl/item/notturnos, ODI0ODE2MjQ/8/#info:metadata.

[2] Zur Zuschreibung dieses Nocturnes vgl.: Jean-Jacques Eigeldinger, *Chopin et la baronne Nathaniel de Rothschild* […], S. 37–40.

[3] Vgl. den Brief an Tytus Woyciechowski vom 15. Mai 1830, *Friedrich Chopins Gesammelte Briefe*, Übers./Hrsg. Bernhard Scharlitt, Leipzig, Breitkopf & Härtel, 1911), S. 76.

[4] Uta Goebl-Streicher: „Frédéric Chopin – Einblick in Unterricht und Umfeld. Die Briefe seiner Lieblingsschülerin Friederike Müller, Paris 1839–1845", in *Musikwissenschaftliche Schriften*, 51 (München-Salzburg, Katzbichler, 2018), Brief Nr. 198, S. 503–505.

[5] In einem Brief an die Familie vom 22. Dezember 1830 erwähnt Chopin dieses Klavier als „cudny" [herrlich, wundervoll], *Korespondencja Fryderyka Chopina* (Warschau, WUW, 2009), Bd. I, S. 453–455. Sydow hat dieses Adjektiv irrtümlich als „nudny" [reizlos] wiedergegeben. Vgl.: *Friedrich Chopins Gesammelte Briefe*, a.a.O., S. 115–119.

[6] Vgl.: https://chopinonline.ac.uk/aco/catalogue/nocturnes-opus-9.

[7] Eine Definition, die auf Liszt zurückgeht, vgl. sein Vorwort zu den *Nocturnes* von John Field („Über John Field's Nocturne", Leipzig, Schuberth & Co.), S. 4. Diese Sammlung existiert in verschiedenen Fassungen, die 1850, 1859, 1863, 1869 und 1876 erschienen sind und 6, 8, 9, 12 und 18 Stücke enthalten.

[8] Von Lenz, der Chopin mit dem Stück „quälte", urteilt: „Das Notturno ist nur ein veredelter, auf interessantere Bässe gepfropfter Field" – eine Meinung, die der Komponist seiner Aussage nach geteilt haben soll. Vgl.: Wilhelm von Lenz, *Die großen Pianoforte-Virtuosen unserer Zeit aus persönlicher Bekanntschaft – Liszt - Chopin - Tausig - Henselt*, S. 41.

Zur Aufführung des Nocturnes op. 9 Nr. 2

Da das Nocturne in den Salons für seine lyrischen und elegischen Qualitäten geschätzt wurde, setzte Chopin die Stücke dieser Gattung häufig auf das Programm seiner seltenen Konzerte. Außerdem gehörten sie zum Repertoire, das seine Schüler zu erlernen hatten. In den Exemplaren von Dubois, Stirling, Jędrzejewicz und Zaleska-Rosengardt finden sich zahlreiche Anmerkungen, Korrekturen und Varianten. Andere sind uns durch die pianistische Tradition überliefert. Außerdem haben Georges Mathias, Thomas D. A. Tellefsen und Carl Mikuli jeweils eigene Ausgaben des Schaffens ihres Lehrers hinterlassen.[9]

Durch ihr vergleichsweise schlichtes Notenbild kontrastiert die Originalfassung von op. 9 Nr. 2 deutlich mit jenem Notentext, der alle heute bekannten Varianten zu diesem Nocturne wiedergibt (siehe S. 6–10 dieser Ausgabe). Aufgrund der Fülle an Verzierungen und Arabesken verlangt letzterer eine besondere Herangehensweise sowie ein pianistisches Können, das den gesteigerten technischen Schwierigkeiten Rechnung trägt. Sie verlocken zwar zum virtuosen Spiel, dürfen sich jedoch keinesfalls nachteilig auf den intimen und sanglichen Charakter auswirken, der in der ursprünglichen Fassung so wunderbar zum Ausdruck kommt. In ihrem bereits in Fußnote 4 zitierten Brief erwähnt Friederike Streicher-Müller, dass ihr der Meister während seiner Unterrichtsstunde am 13. Mai 1841 die Verzierungen in allen Varianten vorgestellt habe, damit sie das Stück genau wie er spielen könne. Entsprach die zu sehr an Field erinnernde Urfassung (vgl. Fußnote 7), die auch weniger geübten Klavierspielern zugänglich ist, vielleicht nicht mehr dem inzwischen verfeinerten Geschmack ihres Schöpfers? Er allein könnte diese Frage beantworten.

Auch wenn die folgenden Bemerkungen von Chopins Schülern heute offensichtlich erscheinen, können sie von Nutzen sein. Mikuli stellt fest, dass beim Studium der Nocturnes „der Schüler [...] den schönen gebundenen Gesangston und das Legato erkennen, lieben und ausführen lernen"[10] solle. Wilhelm von Lenz empfahl der Komponist beim Einstudieren von op. 9 Nr. 2 die Stimmen für die linke Hand gesondert zu üben (indem er sie zunächst auf beide Hände aufteilte), um dadurch eine absolute Regelmäßigkeit der Begleitung zu erreichen. Darauf aufbauend kann sich ein breiter Gesang entfalten, dessen Ausdruck mit jeder variierten Wiederkehr des Themas inniger wird. Den von Friedrich Niecks überlieferten Aussagen Adolf Gutmanns zufolge ließ Chopin seine Schüler die in vielen seiner Werke anzutreffenden Wellenbewegungen der Begleitung sanft und mit halber Lautstärke spielen.[11] Die begabte Pianistin Friederike Streicher-Müller betont ebenfalls, wie wichtig die Regelmäßigkeit und die Unabhängigkeit der linken Hand seien.[12] Wegen der unzureichenden Hinweise zur Dynamik in den Erstausgaben war sie gezwungen, das zweite Nocturne op. 37 siebenmal zu wiederholen, bis es ihren anspruchsvollen Lehrer ganz zufrieden stellte.[13]

Die Metronomangaben zu diesen Werken werfen schwierige Fragen auf. Ab op. 28 finden sie sich weder in den Manuskripten noch in den Druckfassungen. Die Angaben für die ersten acht Nocturnes überraschen dagegen durch ihre Geschwindigkeit. Was op. 9 Nr. 2 betrifft, ist der in den Erstausgaben genannte Richtwert schlicht und einfach falsch („♩" oder „♩." statt „♪"; vgl. dazu auch die Erörterung im Kritischen Bericht). Seit langem wird nicht nur in diesem Werk, sondern auch in den meisten anderen Nocturnes von Chopin ein gemäßigteres Tempo angeschlagen, das nach allgemeiner Auffassung sowohl der Idee des romantischen Lyrismus als auch dem größeren Klangvolumen moderner Instrumente besser gerecht wird.

Raoul Pugno, der am Pariser Konservatorium von Georges Mathias – einem der wenigen professionellen Musiker unter Chopins Schülern – unterrichtet wurde, macht auf eine seinerzeit weitverbreitete und heute noch gepflegte Praxis aufmerksam, wobei er den klugen Rat gibt: „Ich kann nur immer wieder darauf hinweisen, dass beide Hände genau zusammen angeschlagen werden müssen. Es ist wirklich grauenhaft und unmusikalisch, in jedem Takt hören zu müssen, wie die Begleitung vor der Melodienote

erklingt."[14] Eine Bemerkung, die bedacht und vor allem umgesetzt werden sollte.

Bleibt eine wichtige Frage: Ist es möglich, Chopins Nocturnes samt ihrer unzähligen Verzierungen und Arabesken ohne Flexibilität zu interpretieren und dabei die Vorschrift zu befolgen, dass die linke Hand die Bewegung aufs Genaueste einzuhalten hat (also den Kapellmeister darstellt, ein Uhrwerk), während es der rechten erlaubt ist, sich vom Zwang der Metrik zu befreien? Unserer Meinung nach gibt darauf Raoul Koczalski die beste Antwort, die eng mit dem Verständnis des *Tempo rubato*[15] zusammenhängt, obwohl sie der (unmittelbar zuvor zusammengefassten) Ansicht seines Lehrers Carl Mikuli zu widersprechen scheint:

> Das vielumstrittene „Tempo rubato" ist ja nichts anderes als der schnelle, plötzliche Wechsel des rallentando und accellerando [sic!]. Wenn die rechte Hand in zurückhaltender, gedehnter oder beschleunigter Weise die Melodie spielt, muß auch die linke Hand dieselbe Verlangsamung oder Beschleunigung eintreten lassen, und der rechten Hand folgen. Die Noten verteile man so, daß auf jede angeschlagene Note oder jeden Akkord in der linken Hand so und so viele gleich verteilte Noten in der rechten Hand kommen, da beide Hände immer zu gleicher Zeit anschlagen müssen. Nur an einigen Stellen, wo in der rechten Hand Verzierungen vorkommen, wo durch Wärme und Leidenschaftlichkeit des Ausdrucks die rechte Hand sich zögernd oder entschlossen von der linken freimacht, kann ein kaum merklicher Unterschied im Anschlagen der beiden Hände eintreten. Aber derartige Fälle kommen nur äußerst selten vor und sind mit großer Vorsicht anzuwenden.[16]

Die Literatur zu Chopin ist umfangreich. Sein Leben, sein Werk, sein Unterrichten, seine Virtuosität und sein einzigartiger Zugang zum Klavier bilden den Gegenstand ständig neuer wissenschaftlicher Veröffentlichungen, die unsere Kenntnisse erweitern. Doch um sein Genie gebührend würdigen zu können, hätte man zu gerne der Unterrichtsstunde beigewohnt, in der es Emilie von Gretsch vergönnt war, ihren Lehrer zweimal seine Nocturnes spielen zu hören, oder den Platz von Charles Hallé eingenommen, der, nachdem er Chopins Spiel gehört hatte, schrieb: „Es machte mich sprachlos. Ich verlor den letzten Rest an Verstand. Ich wäre imstande gewesen, in die Seine zu springen. [...] Ich kann guten Gewissens versichern, dass niemand jemals fähig gewesen ist, seine Werke so zu spielen, wie sie unter seinen magischen Fingern erklangen".[17]

Weiterführende Literatur

Eigeldinger, Jean-Jacques, *Chopin et la baronne Nathaniel de Rothschild, Nocturne en ut mineur et Valse en la mineur sans numéro d'opus, problèmes d'attribution* (Warschau, NIFC, 2016).
— *Chopin vu par ses élèves* (Paris, Fayard, 2006).
Koczalski, Raoul, *Zum hundertsten Geburtstag Frédéric Chopin : Chopin-Zyklus : Vier Klaviervorträge nebst einer biographischen Skizze : F. Chopin, sowie den Aufsätzen: Chopin als Komponist und Chopin als Pianist, und einer eingehenden Analyse aller zum Vortrag bestimmten Werke* (Leipzig, Pabst, 1909.).
Lenz, Wilhelm von, *Die großen Pianoforte-Virtuosen unserer Zeit aus persönlicher Bekanntschaft – Liszt - Chopin - Tausig - Henselt* (Berlin, B. Behr's Buchhandlung, 1872).
Pugno, Raoul, *Les Leçons écrites de Raoul Pugno, Chopin* (Paris, Librairie des Annales, 1909).
Rink, John, „'Structural Momentum' and Closure in Chopin's Nocturne Op. 9, No. 2", in *Schenker Studies 2*, Hrsg. Carl Schachter und Hedi Siegel (Cambridge, Cambridge University Press, 1999), S. 109–126.

Christophe Grabowski
(Übersetzung: Jan Wolfrum)

Mein besonderer Dank geht an Jean-Jacques Eigeldinger und John Rink für ihre wertvollen Ratschläge bei der Vorbereitung dieser Ausgabe.

---

[9] *Œuvres choisies pour piano par F. Chopin, édition revue et corrigée par G. Mathias* (Paris, Maison Lemoine aîné, Harand successeur, 1859), *Collection des œuvres pour le piano par Frédéric Chopin, en douze livraisons, publiée par T. D. A. Tellefsen* (Paris, Richault 1860), *Fr. Chopin's Pianoforte-Werke, revid. u. m. Fingersatz versehen (zum grössten Theil nach des Autors Notirungen) v. Carl Mikuli* (Leipzig, Kistner, 1879–1880).

[10] Vgl. S. IV des in Fußnote 1 zitierten Vorworts.

[11] Frederick Niecks, *Frederick Chopin as a Man and Musician* (London & New York, Novello, Ewer Co., 1888), Bd. II, S. 264, Fußnote 33 (abrufbar unter https://polona.pl/item/frederick-chopin-as-a-man-and-musician-in-two-volumes-vol-2,MTE4NzEzMA/138/#item).

[12] Uta Goebl-Streicher, „Frédéric Chopin", a.a.O., Briefe Nr. 70 u. 71, S. 121 u. 124. Es geht an dieser Stelle eigentlich um die Nocturnes op. 27, aber das Gesagte lässt sich genauso auf op. 9 Nr. 2 anwenden.

[13] Ebd., Brief Nr. 119, S. 272. Die Manuskripte dieses Werkes, die Chopin seinen Verlegern zukommen ließ, enthielten sehr wenige Unterschiede. Einige davon notierte er im Exemplar Dubois.

[14] Raoul Pugno, *Les Leçons écrites de Raoul Pugno, Chopin*, S. 66. Pugno folgt hierin Thalberg, der diese Gewohnheit ebenfalls anprangert und die „Manier, die Melodie-Noten erst übertrieben lange nach denen der Begleitung anzuschlagen" verurteilt. Doch Thalberg differenziert seine Haltung, denn er ist der Meinung: „Bei einer Melodie, die sich in langsamen Zeitmaasse und in Noten von langer Dauer bewegt, ist es allerdings von guter Wirkung, wenn man namentlich zu Anfang jeden Taktes oder beim Beginn jedes Abschnittes der Melodie, den Gesang erst nach dem Basse eintreten lässt, jedoch nur mit einer fast unmerklichen Verzögerung." Vgl.: Sigismund Thalberg, *Die Kunst des Gesanges auf dem Pianoforte* (Leipzig, Breitkopf & Härtel, 1853), S. 2 (abrufbar unter https://polona.pl/item/choeur-des-conjures-de-l-opera-il-crociato-de-meyerbeer-op-70,MTA0MTY1MTQy/3/#info:metadata). In ihren Chopin-Aufnahmen spielen Pugno und Koczalski entsprechend Thalbergs Empfehlung oft die linke Hand ein klein wenig vor der rechten. Dennoch stellt Koczalski mit Pugno fest: „Beide Hände sollen die Tasten gleichzeitig mit peinlicher Genauigkeit anschlagen", vgl.: Raoul Koczalski, *Zum hundertsten Geburtstag Frédéric Chopin*, S. 26.

[15] Diese Bezeichnung, die sonst hauptsächlich in volkstümlichen Kontexten gebraucht wird, findet sich in den Nocturnes lediglich zweimal: in op. 9 Nr. 2 (Takt 26) und in op. 15 Nr. 3 (Takt 1). Dabei ist erwähnenswert, dass im Exemplar Stirling beim zweiten der genannten Werke das *languido* als auch das genannte *rubato* ausgestrichen wurden.

[16] Raoul Koczalski, *Zum hundertsten Geburtstag Frédéric Chopin*, S. 27.

[17] Jean-Jacques Eigeldinger, *Chopin vu par ses élèves*, S. 111, 343–344.

* * *

Nocturne
(Original version)

Op. 9 No. 2

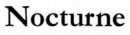

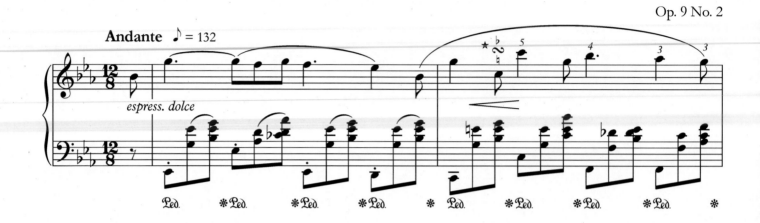

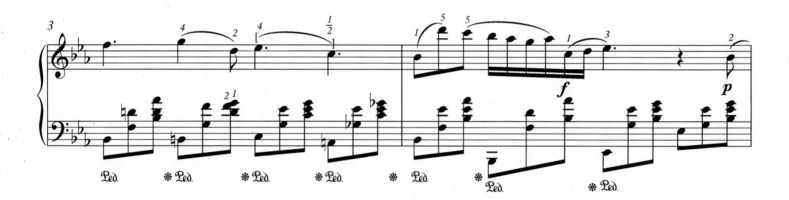

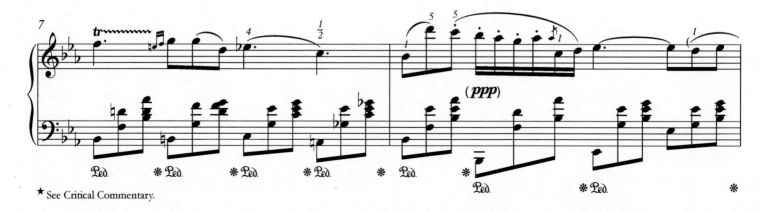

★ See Critical Commentary.

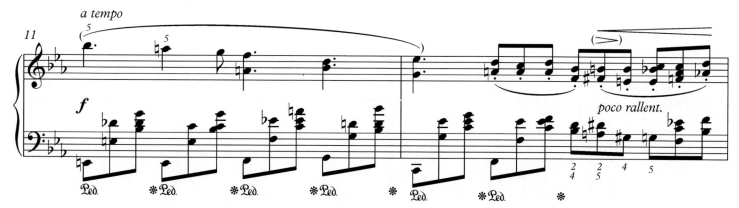

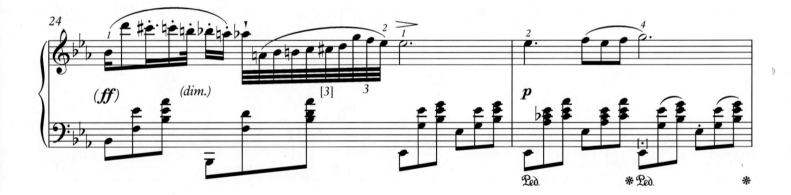

★ See Critical Commentary.

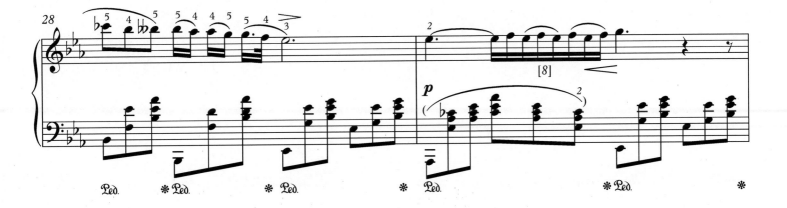

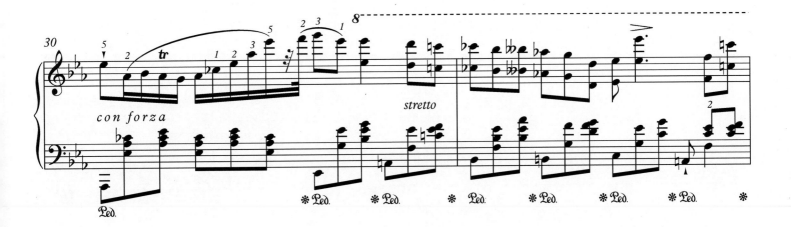

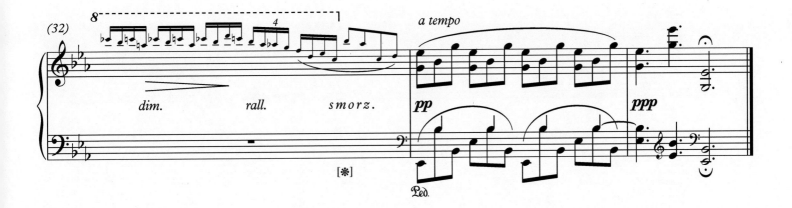

Nocturne
(Version with variants based on M²)★

Op. 9 No. 2

Gesangsvoll, mit grossem Ton
(*Cantabile, con suono*)

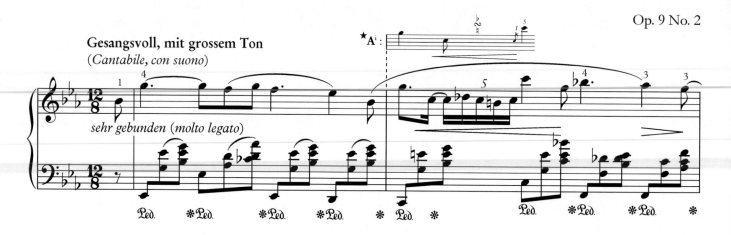

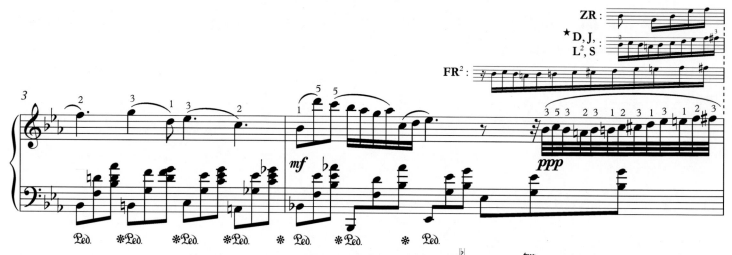

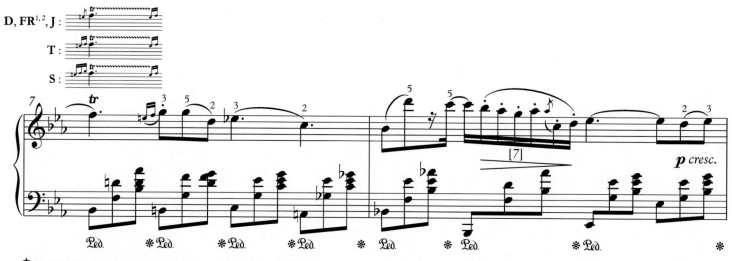

★ See Critical Commentary for the variants preceded by an asterisk.

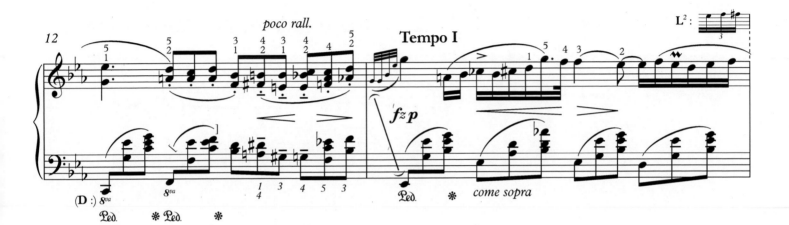

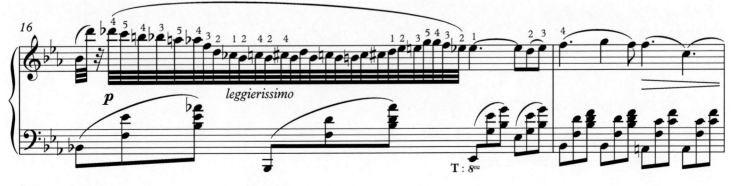

★ See Critical Commentary.

★ See Critical Commentary.

★★ The trill should begin slowly and then become faster.

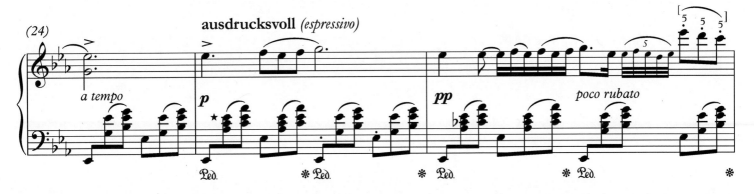

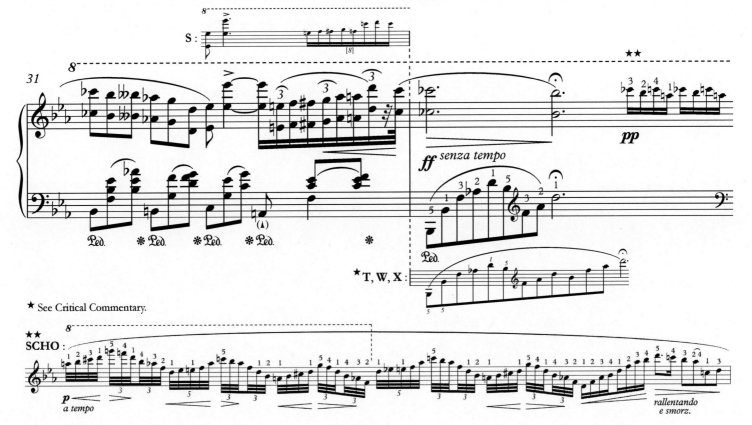

★ See Critical Commentary.

★★★ See Critical Commentary.

NOTES ON EDITORIAL METHOD AND PRACTICE

Editorial concept

The Complete Chopin is based on two key premises. First, there can be no definitive version of Chopin's works: variants form an integral part of the music. Second, a permissive conflation of readings from several sources – in effect producing a version of the music that never really existed – should be avoided. Accordingly, our procedure is to identify a single principal source for each work and to prepare an edition of that source (which we regard as 'best', even if it cannot be definitive). At the same time, we reproduce important variants from other authorized sources either adjacent to or, in certain instances, within the main music text, in footnotes or in the Critical Commentary, thus enabling scholarly comparison and facilitating choice in performance. (Conflation may be inadmissible for the editor, but it remains an option and right for the performer.) Multiple versions of whole works are presented when differences between the sources are so abundant or fundamental that they go beyond the category of 'variant'.

Sources

The complexity of the Chopin sources could hardly be greater, given the varying ways in which each work was drafted, prepared for publication (usually in three different countries) and subsequently revised in successive impressions. Our edition takes account of the following sources as relevant:

- autograph manuscripts, many of which were used by engravers (i.e. *Stichvorlagen*, or engraver's manuscripts);
- proofs, whether uncorrected or corrected by Chopin;
- first editions, including subsequent impressions released during Chopin's lifetime if relevant;
- autograph glosses in the scores of his students and associates; and
- editions of pieces for which no other source material survives.

In determining a single principal source for each piece, we have been guided by several factors of variable relevance from work to work. For the music published during Chopin's lifetime, these include the following:

- Chopin's presence in Paris, which allowed him to correct proofsheets and successive impressions of the French first edition, whereas he had less control over the publication process in Germany and England. We therefore tend to privilege the French first edition and later printings thereof;
- the existence of an autograph or authoritative copy related to a particular first edition; and
- the quality of the source with respect to errors and clarity of presentation.

For the posthumously published works, a more *ad hoc* methodology must be adopted, taking into account extant autograph manuscripts or approved copies or early editions when no other source material survives. The rationale for the selection of each work's principal source is given in the Critical Commentary.

Editorial principles

Our central aim is fidelity to the designated principal source except when errors and omissions occur therein. When such errors and omissions are indisputable, corrections are made tacitly in the music text, without distinguishing marks, but are discussed in the Critical Commentary (except for certain types of accidental; see below). When they are open to debate, any changes made editorially are distinguished in the music text by the use of square brackets; the Critical Commentary will discuss and justify these changes as necessary.

When other authorized sources offer significant alternatives, we present these as variants in one of the following ways:

- *alternative music text* is positioned on the page, either next to the main text or in footnotes; the provenance of each variant is identified according to the system of abbreviations defined in the Critical Commentary;
- *alternative dynamics, articulation and other small-scale variants* are incorporated within the music text but are distinguished by round brackets;
- *alternative fingerings* are printed in italics; and
- *alternative pedallings* appear below the staff in smaller type and enclosed within round brackets, their provenance being identified according to the system of abbreviations defined in the Critical Commentary.

Minor alternatives in other authorized sources are discussed and reproduced in the Critical Commentary as necessary, but do not appear in the body of the edition proper.

The principle of fidelity to an early nineteenth-century source raises important questions about the appearance of our Edition, given the differences in notational conventions between Chopin's age and our own. Our general practice is to conserve relevant features of early to mid nineteenth-century notation while modernizing details which otherwise would not be comprehensible to today's performers. The criterion is whether or not a given feature has any bearing on the music's meaning. For instance, we generally follow the original notation with regard to the position of slurs before or after tied notes; the chains of small-scale slurs in Chopin's original texts; superimposed (multiple) slurs; unbroken beamings across multiple groups of quavers, semiquavers etc.; and the disposition of the hands across the staves. We also respect the expressive idiosyncrasies of parallel passages.

Select characteristics of the Edition

- *Square brackets* distinguish all editorial interventions except precautionary accidentals (which are added only when reading accuracy is jeopardized). *Round brackets* (parentheses) designate additions and variants from other authorized sources.
- *Accidentals* missing from the original source are tacitly replaced in this Edition when these are found within the same bar at a higher or lower register, and when they clearly apply to other uses of the same pitch class in that bar (this sort of omission being extremely typical of Chopin).
- No editorial *fingerings* have been added. When Chopin's own fingerings appear in the principal source, they are presented in roman type in our Edition. Any significant fingerings from other authorized sources appear in italics; their provenance is identified in the Critical Commentary.
- *Right- and left-hand parts* may be divided between the two staves when such a disposition is vital to the original sense or better conforms to hand positions. This is how Chopin tended to notate his music, and it may be significant with regard to articulation and sonority.
- *Accents* pose a major problem in Chopin editing. Accents of various sizes are found throughout Chopin's manuscripts (as well as many scribal copies) and apparently have different meanings according to context; nevertheless, such meanings can be difficult to ascertain, not least because of notational inconsistencies on Chopin's part which make the editor's job all the more vexed. This Edition preserves the two principal types of accent in Chopin's autographs: conventional accents (>) and 'long accents' ($\Longrightarrow$). The latter seem to have various functions: to indicate dynamic reinforcement, expressive stress and proportional prolongation for notes of long rhythmic value (i.e. minims and semibreves); to convey a sense

of 'leaning' to appoggiaturas, suspensions and syncopations; to emphasize groups of two, three or four notes, as well as rolled chords; and to prolong a stress over tied notes. Long accents are best thought of as a 'surge', versus the dynamic retraction implied by a visually similar diminuendo sign (with which many early and modern Chopin editions alike replace the long accents intended by Chopin). Marcato accents (∧, as opposed to >) are retained from the original.

- This Edition presents both *grace notes* (with stroke) and *'long appoggiaturas'* (without stroke), thus preserving a distinction clearly intended by Chopin.
- A flexible approach to *stem directions* on a single staff has been taken. Standard modern practice is not observed when the original stem directions convey a meaning that modernized notation would lack.
- *Liaisons* (i.e. diagonal lines) between the hands are reproduced where relevant; taken from the copies of Chopin's students (especially those of Camille Dubois), these indicate a simultaneous attack on the beat with both hands.
- *Rests* are added only when the original sense is unclear or in cases of error or omission.
- *Pedalling.* Where a ℘ marking or pedal release (✱) is either erroneous or absent, and when its placement is unambiguous, such an indication is inserted without square brackets but is discussed in the Critical Commentary; when its placement is open to debate, any editorial correction or addition will be designated by square brackets, with justification provided in the Critical Commentary as necessary. In general, pedal releases are not added at the ends of pieces: the pedalling remains 'open' in keeping with Chopin's practice.
- *Triplets* and similar rhythmic groupings are indicated with small numbers. Such groupings and similar ornamental shapes are not slurred as a matter of policy, as such slurs in Chopin's music often designate legato articulation, not rhythmic grouping. We therefore follow his notational practice.
- Elements in the principal source deemed to be superfluous (e.g. redundant accidentals, pedal releases, slurs, and staccato or augmentation dots) are not retained in this Edition; the Critical Commentary will discuss only those elements which are open to debate.

Critical Commentary

The Critical Commentary identifies the particular strategy for the choice of primary and secondary sources, provides information on sources (including dates and library sigla as necessary) and justifies individual decisions regarding the text. It also reports on relevant variants and corrections of errors and omissions in the principal source. The identification of obvious mistakes and faulty notation in the sources is avoided; so too is the description of secondary musical details in subsidiary sources.

Standard library sigla are given as relevant for manuscript material. The following abbreviations are used when necessary:

RH = right hand
LH = left hand
Br. = brass
Str. = strings
Ww. = woodwind; plus standard abbreviations for other orchestral instruments.

To specify pitches, the Helmholtz system is used as follows:

An oblique (/) is used for comments applying to more than one part (e.g. 'RH/LH' refers to both RH and LH). Commas are used in succession when a given feature occurs in a number of bars or sources (e.g. 'Bars 6, 7, 8. > to RH note 2 from **F**') or when a given element has multiple features (e.g. 'Bar 19. **p**, > to LH chord 1 from **S**').

This Edition employs a precise and unambiguous means of identifying individual notes and chords within a bar. In general, these are referred to in the Critical Commentary with regard to their position as an *event* within a given bar. For instance, in the following music example (the first bar from the E minor Concerto Op. 11):

'w' = bar 1 RH note 3, as it is a single note and the third right-hand event in the bar;

'x' = bar 1 RH chord 4, as it is a chord (i.e. two or more notes) and the fourth right-hand event in the bar;

'y' = bar 1 LH note 2, as it is a single note and the second left-hand event in the bar; and

'z' = bar 1 LH chord 3, as it is a chord (i.e. two or more notes) and the third left-hand event in the bar.

Acknowledgements

Financial support for *The Complete Chopin* has been generously provided by the Arts and Humanities Research Council, the British Academy, the British Council, the Swiss National Science Foundation, and the Department of Music, Royal Holloway, University of London.

John Rink
Jim Samson
Jean-Jacques Eigeldinger
Christophe Grabowski

CRITICAL COMMENTARY

NOCTURNE OP. 9 NO. 2

Original version

Sources

A^i   Autograph-incipit of first two RH bars, dated '22 Sept. Drezno 1835', presented to Maria Wodzińska, now lost, reproduced in Leopold Binental, *Chopin, w 120-tą rocznicę urodzin: Dokumenty i pamiątki* (Warsaw: Łazarski, 1930), plate 51.[1]

F^1   French first edition, published 20 December 1832 within *Album des Pianistes*. M. Schlesinger, Paris, plate no. M. S. 1287.*

F^2   Corrected reprint of **F^1**, published as separate edition early 1833.

F^3   Corrected reprint of **F^2**, published c. 1846–47 by Schlesinger's successor Brandus & Co.

F^4   Corrected reprint of **F^3**, c. 1854–59.[2]

G^1   German first edition, January 1833. Fr. Kistner, Leipzig, plate no. 995.*

G^2   Corrected reprint of **G^1**, before 1841.

E   Reprint of English first edition, late 1840 (first impression unlocated, published mid 1833). Wessel & Co., London, plate no. (W & C° N° 916.).

D   Dubois copy of **F^2**. [F-Pn: Rés. F. 980 (II, 1)]

FR^1   Franchomme copy of **F^2**. [France, private collection][3]

FR^2   Franchomme copy of **F^4**, published 1875 by Brandus et Cie. [A-Wn: S.H. Chopin 35]

J   Jędrzejewicz copy of **F^2**. [PL-Wmfc: M/174]

S   Stirling copy of **F^2**. [F-Pn: Rés. Vma 241 (I, 9)]

T   Annotated copy of **G^1**. [PL-Tu: IV 5439 Cim.]

W   Annotated copy c. 1848 of reprint of **F^3**. [PL-Wbfc: 1662/n]

X   Annotated copy of **F^2**.[4]

ZR   Zaleska-Rozengardt copy of **F^2**. [PL-Wmfc: MC/307]

*   The first editions are abbreviated '**F**', '**G**' except when referring only to specific impressions (i.e. **F^1**, **F^2**, **F^3**, **F^4**, **G^1** or **G^2**).

Suggested filiation

The French first edition (**F^1**) – prepared on the basis of a manuscript now lost – initially appeared in the *Album des Pianistes*, prior to the release some weeks later of a corrected, separately published version (**F^2**). **F^1** served as the *Stichvorlage* of the English first edition (**E**). The German first edition (**G^1**) also seems to have been based on **F^1**, although it includes a number of corrections of obvious errors that were redressed in **F^2**. Before their publication, both **G^1** and **E** were revised by respective house proof-readers.

---

[1] Incipit can be viewed at https://archive.org/details/ChopinDokumentyPamiatki/page/n77/mode/1up, no. 51.

[2] The annotations in the exemplar of **F^4** reproduced on the US-Cu website (shelfmark M25.C54 N5902 c.1) and in OCVE are not considered here; the emendations in question correspond to those in **S** (specifically, in b. 21) and **D**. One variant is unique to this score: eb^2 (grace note with fingering '1'), added after RH note 9 in bar 26 by analogy to bar 2.

[3] It has not been possible to consult **FR^1** while preparing this edition; reference has therefore been made to the discussion of this source in Jean-Jacques Eigeldinger, *Chopin vu par ses élèves* (Paris: Fayard, 2006), pp. 283–288, 326–330.

[4] For information see Jeffrey Kallberg, 'Sense and Meaning in Two Recently Discovered Editions Annotated by Chopin', in *Chopin in Paris: The 1830s*, ed. Artur Szklener (Warsaw: NIFC, 2006), pp. 331–342.

As the foregoing source list demonstrates, each of these editions was corrected during Chopin's lifetime, and further refinements were made after his death in 1849. The 'definitive' corrected reprint of the French edition first appeared in c. 1854 (**F^4**). A first corrected reprint of the English first edition was published around 1852; a second followed in c. 1856–57, while a final corrected version appeared some time after 1860. The editorial history of the German prints was the most complex of all. Instead of making ongoing ameliorations to the original plates, Kistner chose to publish two newly engraved editions of Nocturnes 1 and 3, with no fewer than four new editions of the especially popular second Nocturne (which was also marketed separately). The Annotated Catalogue Online (www.chopinonline.ac.uk/aco) traces the complete evolution of the printed sources for Op. 9, most of which are reproduced in the Online Chopin Variorum Edition (www.chopinonline.ac.uk/ocve).

Given the absence of a manuscript and the presence of numerous imperfections in all of the first editions, **F^3** – the last to have been corrected during the composer's lifetime – serves as the basis of this edition.

Principal source: **F^3**

Bar 0.   All printed sources: inaccurate MM indication '♩ = 132'; **T**: '♩' corrected by hand to '♪' (as here)

Bar 2.   Turn to RH note 2: ∽ in F; ∼ in G; ↝ in **A^i**, **E**. In his manuscripts Chopin tended to notate a turn (*gruppetto*) by using the symbol ↝ or, exceptionally, ∼, in both cases indicating a descending turn.[5] Notwithstanding the notation in **F**, he generally did not employ the symbol for an ascending turn, i.e. ∽ or ∾;[6] instead, he wrote out such ornaments in small notes in certain pieces. According to Clive Brown, the sign ↝ could indicate either a trill followed by a turn or a close turn (i.e. with an accidental before the first and/or third notes).[7] In the printed sources of this Nocturne, the turn sign in bar 2 appears above the note, which for a close turn would yield [music example] (as per **F**), [music example] (as per **E**), [music example] (as per **G**; the engraver of which omitted the vertical line present in the *Stichvorlage* – i.e. **F^1** – or did not grasp its meaning). However, some authors like Pierre Baillot and Charles de Bériot[8] mention that this kind of turn could be started on the main note, which would yield

---

[5] Chopin's habit of notating turn signs without specifying the necessary accidentals therein was somewhat old-fashioned. He thus left it to individual performers to decide the precise realization of the turns, presumably in accordance with the prevailing convention whereby the notes of a *gruppetto* span either a minor third or a diminished third, depending on context. An explicit form of notation with accidentals indicated above and/or below a turn was nevertheless widely used by that time; see for example the general guidelines in François-Joseph Fétis, *Solfèges progressifs avec accompagnement de piano précédés des principes de la musique* (Paris: M. Schlesinger, c. 1837), p. 25. This notation appears (albeit inaccurately) in the first editions of the Concerto Op. 11 (viewable at www.chopinonline.ac.uk/cfeo): see movement II, bar 31.

[6] The ascending turn is also present in bar 26 of this Nocturne (see comment below) and in bars 31, 98 of the second movement of the Concerto Op. 11 (French first edition).

[7] Clive Brown, *Classical and Romantic Performing Practice* (Oxford, Oxford University Press, 1999), p. 513. Brown comments furthermore (pp. 503, 506, 507) on the confusion surrounding both the notation and the interpretation of this sign, which vary between composers.

[8] Pierre Baillot, *L'art du violon. Nouvelle méthode dédiée à ses élèves* (Paris: Dépôt central de la musique et de la librairie, c. 1834), p. 84 (https://gallica.bnf.fr/ark:/12148/bpt6k11638868/f98); Charles de Bériot, *Méthode de violon divisée en 3 parties, Op. 102* (Paris: de Bériot, 1857), p. 188 (https://gallica.bnf.fr/ark:/12148/bpt6k1163701t/f226).

[musical notation] (as per **F**), [musical notation] (as per **E**). In **Aⁱ**, the turn sign ~ appears between RH notes 2 and 3, clearly indicating that the ornament should be played as in the last version specified for **E**. Here the notation in **F** is changed to ∾ with reference to the realization suggested in **Aⁱ**. Accidentals are added by hand to the turn in select sources: ♭ (for d♭²) in **D**, **FR²**, **T**; ♮ (for b♮¹) in **D**, **FR²**. Fingering to RH notes 3, 5 from **ZR**; to RH notes 6, 7 from **S**. Fingerings not reproduced here: '4' for d♭² in turn in **T**, '3' for RH note 2 in **ZR**.

Bar 3. Fingering to RH note 2 from **ZR** (also in **FR¹**); to RH note 3 from **ZR**; to RH note 4 from **D** (also in **FR¹**, **J**, **S**, **T**, **ZR**); to RH note 5 from **S** (upper fingering), **D** (lower fingering, also in **T**, **ZR**). Fingering to upper notes LH chord 6 from **D**. Slur to RH notes 4–5 by analogy with bar 7. Precautionary ♮ to upper note LH chord 2 also present in **FR²**, **G²**.

Bar 4. Fingering to RH notes 2, 3 from **D** (also in **FR¹**, **J**, **S**, **ZR**); to RH note 8 from **D** (also in **S**, **ZR**); to RH note 10 from **D**, **ZR**; to RH note 11 from **S**. **FR²**: *f* (printed under RH note 7) rubbed out and placed under RH note 2 (**S**: additional *f* under RH note 10); here under RH note 8 in accordance with melodic phrasing (**G** as here).

Bar 5. All sources: *p* under RH note 1, not bar 4 RH note 11 as here (i.e. at beginning of new phrase). Fingering from **S** (**W**: '1' added above RH note 2, not reproduced here).

Bar 6. **F¹⁻³**, **G**, **E**: no ♭s to RH note 4 (added by hand in **D**, **J**, **S**; see also **F⁴**), RH note 10 (added by hand in **S**; see also **F⁴**). Precautionary ♭ to RH note 13 also present in **E**, **FR²**. Fingering to RH notes 10, 11 from **D**, **FR¹**, **J**, **S**; to RH notes 12, 13 from **S**.

Bars 6, 22. **F**: size of accents to RH notes 4–5, 6–7, 8–9 ambiguous; here long accents in accordance with Chopin's notational habits at the time (cf. e.g. Concerto Op. 21)

Bar 7. **F¹⁻³**, **G**, **E**: no ♮ to RH note 2 (added by hand in **J**; see also **F⁴**). **F**, **G**, **E**: no ♭ to RH note 7 (added by hand in **FR²**). Fingering to RH note 7 from **D** (see also **S**, **T**); to RH note 8 from **S** (upper fingering), **D**, **T** (lower fingering).

Bar 8. Fingering to RH notes 1–3, 9 from **D**; to RH note 13 from **S** (see also **T**, **ZR**). *ppp* from **S**.

Bars 8–9. RH slur over barline from **E**

Bar 9. Fingering to RH note 1 from **J**, **S**; to RH note 2 from **FR¹**

Bar 10. Fingering to RH notes 5, 7, 10 from **T**; to RH notes 8, 9 from **J**, **T**

Bar 11. **F**, **G¹**, **E**: no ♮ to upper note LH chord 11 (added by hand in **FR²**; see also **G²**). **G**: upper notes LH chords 9, 12 respectively f¹, g¹; corrected to a¹, bb¹ in **T**. Fingering to RH note 1 from **T**; to RH note 2 from **J**. **F**, **G**, **E**: no ♮ to lower note LH chord 2 (added by hand in **D**). Precautionary ♭ to upper note LH chord 8 also present in **G**.

Bars 11–12. RH slur over barline from **S**

Bar 12. **D**, **J**: vertical line added in pencil after RH/LH chord 5, probably indicating a 'breath', i.e. slight pause, more emphatic than conventional break between successive phrases. Long accent to RH chord 6 from **S** (see also **T**, **ZR**). Fingering from **S**.

Bar 13. Slur to RH notes 1–3 from **E** (see also bar 21). Fingering to RH note 7 from **J**, **S**; to RH note 10 from **S**. Liaison to LH/RH beat 1 from **D**.

Bars 13–15. RH slur over barlines from **J**

Bar 14. **F¹⁻³**, **G**: no ♭ to RH note 10 (added by hand in **D**, **S**, **FR²**; see also **F⁴**; erroneous ♮ in **E**). Precautionary ♭ to RH note 13 also present in **G**, **E**, **FR²**. Fingering from **D**. **E**: *ff* on beat 7.

Bar 15. Fingering from **J**

Bar 15, 23. **F**, **G**, **E**: no ♮ to RH note 2 (see **F⁴**), no ♭ to RH note 7 (added by hand in **FR²**). Slur to RH notes 7–8 from **E** (see also bar 7). Precautionary ♮ to upper note LH chord 2 also present in **G²**.

Bar 16. **F**, **G¹**, **E**: RH notes 4–15 notated incorrectly as semiquavers (**G²** as here). **F¹,²**, **E**: lower note LH chord 5 d; corrected to f in **G**, **F³** and by hand in **D**, **J**, **S**, **X**. Fingering to RH note 11 from **J**, **S**.

Bar 17. Fingering from **J**

Bar 18. Fingering from **S**, **T**

Bar 19. **F**, **G**, **E**: no ♮s to lower note LH chord 2, upper note LH chord 11 (see comment to bar 11). Fingering from **T**. Precautionary ♭ to upper note LH chord 8 also present in **W**.

Bars 19–20. RH slur over barline from **S**. **S** contains another annotation which is difficult to interpret (and thus is not reproduced here), most likely a pencilled *ff* straddling the barline.

Bar 20. **D**: vertical line added in pencil after RH/LH chord 5 as in bar 12 (see comment to bar 12); slur added in **T** to LH chords 8–12 (not reproduced here) has similar function. **T**: line added in pencil between d♯¹ LH chord 7, e♭¹ RH chord 7 to show voice-leading connection between LH/RH. Fingering from **T**.

Bar 21. Liaison to LH/RH beat 1 from **D**. Slur to LH chords 2–3 from **E**.

Bars 21–22. Slur from bar 21 RH note 1 to bar 22 RH note 1 from **ZR**

Bar 22. **F¹⁻³**, **G**: no ♭ to RH note 10 (added by hand in **D**; see also **F⁴**; erroneous ♮ in **E**). Precautionary ♭ to RH note 14 also present in **G**, **FR²**. Fingering from **D**. Slur to LH chords 5–6 from **E**.

Bar 23. Fingering from **J**

Bar 24. Prolongation dot to RH note 3: omitted in **G¹**, added to RH note 4 in **G²** (**F**, **E** as here). **S**: wavy line drawn in pencil over RH notes 13–17, suggesting written-out ritardando (not reproduced here). Fingering to RH note 1 from **S**, **X**; to RH note 17 from **W**; to RH note 18 from **D**, **W**. *ff* from **S**. *dim.* from **E**.

Bar 25. Fingering to RH note 1 from **S**, **W**; to RH note 5 from **S**. Staccato dot to LH note 7 by analogy with LH note 10.

Bar 26. Turn to RH note 9: **F**: ∾ (originally ∾? NB apparent vestiges of vertical stroke slightly to right); **G**: ∾; **E**: ~ (possibly reflecting original ∾ in **F**); ∾ here intended as correction of probably erroneous notation in **F** and **E** (see comment to bar 2). According to the advice of Fétis cited above (see p. 13 n. 5), this ornament should be realized either as d²–e♭²–f²–e♭² (if the sign in **F** is interpreted as an ascending turn) or as f²–e♭²–d²–e♭² (as per **G**, **E**), in each case without starting on the e♭². The realization suggested above for bar 2 (i.e. descending turn, beginning on $e\flat^2$) is recommended here. Fingering: to RH note 1 from **W**; to RH note 8 from **S**; to RH note 9 from **W** (upper fingering), **S** (lower fingering).

Bar 27. Fingering from **W**

Bar 28. **T**: slur to LH beats 7–12 (not reproduced here)

Bar 29. **G**, **E**: slur to RH notes 3–6, not RH notes 4–6 as in **F**. Fingering to RH note 1 from **S**, **T**; to top note LH chord 6 from **W**. LH slur beats 1–6 from **T**. In **W**, the *p* on beat 1 (present in all sources) is changed by hand to *ff*, the result of which would be the sustaining of the work's most extreme dynamic level over four bars (note the subsequent *ff* in bar 32); if any such change was to be made, then *f* would have been more appropriate, yielding a logical progression through *con forza* and *stretto* in bar 30 to *ff* in bar 32.

Bar 30. All sources: slurs to both RH notes 11–13 and RH notes 12–13 (as one of these is likely to be redundant, only the longer slur, to RH notes 11–13, is retained here); no ♮ to bottom note LH chord 12. **F**, **G**: long accent situated slightly to right of RH chord 14, not centred as here (also in **E**). **T**: indecipherable annotation above RH chord 14 (probably fingering, either '5' or possibly '1'), not reproduced here. Fingering to RH notes 1, 2 from **D**, **S**; to RH note 7 from **D**, **FR¹**; to RH note 8 from **FR¹**; to RH note 9 from **FR¹**, **T**; to RH note 10 from **D** (see also **FR¹**, **T**, **X**); to RH note 11 from **D** (see also **FR¹**, **S**, **T**, **W**, **X**); to RH note 12 from **FR¹**(see also **T**, **X**); to RH note 13 from **FR¹**(see also **T**, **W**). Precautionary ♮s to RH chord 16 also present in **E**, **FR²**.

Bar 31. **F**: no ♭ to lower note RH chord 1 (added by hand in **FR²**; see also **G**, **E**). **F**, **G**: no ♮s to RH chord 10 (**E** as here). Fingering from **W**.

Bar 32. Fingering to RH from **FR¹**; to LH note 1 from **D** (see also **J**, **S**, **T**, **X**); to LH note 2 from **D** (see also **FR²**, **J**, **S**, **T**, **X**); to LH notes 3, 5, 9 from **J**; LH to note 4 from **J**, **X**; to LH note 6 from **D** (see also **J**, **S**)

Bar 33. **F**: no crotchet stem to LH note 5 (cf. LH notes 2, 8, 11; **G**, **E** as here)

Bar 34. **F**: prolongation dot missing to RH/LH chord 3 (**G**, **E** as here)

Version with variants

Complementary sources

K Jan Kleczyński, *Chopin w celniejszych swoich utworach* (Warsaw: Echo, 1886), p. 20.[9]

L¹ Variants inscribed by Chopin on sheet of music paper intended for Wilhelm von Lenz, presented by the latter to Princess Marcelina Czartoryska in 1850. [US-PHu: Misc Mss (Large) Box 1 Folder 22][10]

L² Wilhelm von Lenz, 'Uebersichtliche Beurtheilung der Pianoforte-Compositionen von Chopin, als Prodromus eines kritischen Katalogs seiner sämmtlichen Werke', *Neue Berliner Musikzeitung*, 26/38 (18 September 1872), p. [297].[11]

---

[9] Variant can be viewed in Polish version at https://polona.pl/item/1192426/11 (p. 20), in English version (London: Reeves, 1896) at https://polona.pl/item/1192671/22 (p. 37), and in German version (Leipzig: Breitkopf & Härtel, 1898) at https://polona.pl/item/1192680/20 (p. 20).

[10] This manuscript is discussed and reproduced in Eigeldinger, *Chopin vu par ses élèves*, plate 21 and p. 197 note 209a.

[11] Text can be viewed at https://digipress.digitale-sammlungen.de/view/bsb11034544_00307_u001/1.

M¹ Chopin, *Nocturnes*, edited and with fingering by Carl Mikuli, January 1879. Fr. Kistner, Leipzig, plate nos. 5271–5270.

M² Chopin, Nocturne Op. 9 No. 2, with the composer's variants, edited by Carl Mikuli, October 1885. Fr. Kistner, Leipzig, plate no. 6640.[12]

SCHO Chopin, Nocturne Op. 9 No. 2, with variants, edited by Hermann Scholtz, January 1899. Peters, Leipzig, plate no. 8522.[13]

The principal source for this version is **M²**.

Note

Not only is this nocturne the most well known of Chopin's works in the genre, but it stands out from the others because of the truly remarkable number of variants to have flowed from Chopin's pen after the work was initially composed. The status of the manifold variants is determined by their respective origins. The authenticity of those in the autograph incipit (**Aⁱ**), the leaf offered to Princess Marcelina Czartoryska by Wilhelm von Lenz (**L¹**), and the scores used by Chopin's students (**D**, **S**, **ZR**) and owned by his sister Ludwika Jędrzejewicz (**J**) lies beyond doubt.[14] In contrast, the provenance of the annotations in certain other scores – namely, **FR¹**, **T**, **W**, **X** – has not yet been fully determined, which means that these variants must be treated with circumspection. Several late nineteenth-century publications, among them the article by von Lenz (**L²**), the late reprint of the French first edition annotated by Auguste Franchomme (**FR²**),[15] the edition of Carl Mikuli (**M²**), the book by Jan Kleczyński (**K**) and finally the edition of Hermann Scholtz (**SCHO**)[16] contain further variants whose origins cannot always be traced.

Irrespective of their status, the present edition encompasses all currently known variants. Pianists who wish to use them in their performances are advised to proceed judiciously and above all not to overburden the music, as doing so would smother the finely calibrated ornamentation of Chopin's original inspiration.

The principal source in use here – **M²** – was based on the version published in the Nocturnes volume in Mikuli's edition (**M¹**). In addition to the fingerings attributable to Chopin, many of which are identical to those in **D**, **J**, **S** and **ZR** (note the italicized fingering in the music text of the original version as well as the Critical Commentary above), **M²** includes 'supplementary' fingerings which are also reproduced here. Variants in **Aⁱ**, **D**, **FR¹,²**, **J**, **K**, **L¹,²**, **S**, **T**, **W**, **X** and **ZR** which do not appear in Mikuli's edition are shown either above or below the

---

[12] Exemplar reproduced on the OCVE website.

[13] For reproductions see Raoul Koczalski, *Frédéric Chopin, Conseils d'interprétation*, pp. 137–141.

[14] Numerous similarities between the annotations in **J** and **S** are detailed by Jean-Jacques Eigeldinger in *Chopin vu par ses élèves*, pp. 278–282.

[15] This score was part of the documentation used to prepare the collected edition of Breitkopf & Härtel published in 1878–79. According to Jean-Jacques Eigeldinger (*Chopin vu par ses élèves*, pp. 286, 326, 327), the earlier print of the French first edition in the Franchomme collection – i.e. **FR¹** – contained only two annotations pertaining to the execution of ornaments in bars 7 and 15 (identical to those in **FR²**). The additional variants present in **FR²** most likely derive from other annotated scores seen by Franchomme.

[16] Scholtz was heavily influenced by Mikuli's edition (**M²**). One variant, probably taken from Kleczyński, appears in a similar location in Scholtz's edition (see comment to bar 16), whereas another in bar 32 with no known counterpart is of more doubtful authenticity (as discussed, for example, by Jean-Jacques Eigeldinger in Raoul Koczalski, *Frédéric Chopin, Conseils d'Interprétation*, p. 26 note 24).

principal text or at the bottom of the page. Any concordances between the variants found in **M²**, the annotated scores and **SCHO** are indicated in the Critical Commentary below.

Chopin notated a number of variants in abbreviated form, using short strokes, wavy lines, etc.; some of these features are all but illegible, making it difficult to determine his intentions. In such cases only a single transcription is given.[17] A clearer sense of their original appearance and possible meaning can be gained by consulting the OCVE website, which has digital scans of most of the annotated scores.

Questions arise from certain details in the principal source (see comments to bars 8–9, 18–20, 27, 34–36), which is also the only one to modify the tonal structure of the accompaniment (see comments to bars 10, 25 & 29). Furthermore, there is no tempo marking, despite the 'Andante. ♪ = 132' specified in **M¹**. Mikuli undoubtedly considered it necessary to adopt a distinctly slower tempo when performing the Nocturne with so many *fioriture*, hence the freedom from metronomic constraint implied by the *ad libitum* marking. He also adds numerous supplementary performance indications (to do with the rhythmic treatment, dynamics, accentuation, etc.) as well as some terms in German which are accompanied here by the equivalent in Italian (in bars 0–1, 25). The note at the bottom of the page concerning the trill in bar 23 (also applicable to the trills in bars 7 and 15) has been translated from German into English. Finally, concerning the differentiation of short and long accents (the latter of which are often construed by editors as decrescendo markings), Mikuli follows **M¹**, in which the long accents have been replaced either by short accents or by diminuendo hairpins.

RH variants specific only to **M²** and **SCHO**: bar 2 (beats 1–3); bar 8 (beats 3–6), bars 14, 16 (beats 1–6); bars 22, 24, 34–36 (beats 1–12); bar 26 (beats 1–3, 6–9), bar 31 (beat 10–12). RH variants specific only to **M²**: bar 15 (beats 1, 3), bar 23 (beat 1). LH variants specific only to **M²**: bar 10 (beats 5, 6), bar 25 (beates 2, 3, 5, 6), bar 29 (beats 2–6).

Bar 2. Variant from **A¹**: descending turn notated as ∿ (here ∾ with ♭ and ♮; these essential accidentals are respectively present in **D, FR², T** and **D, FR²**); note 3 (i.e. grace note) also present in **D, J, S, T, ZR**; fingering to note 3 from **T**, to note 4 from **ZR**. See also comments to original version.

Bar 4. Variant attributed to **D, J, S** notated in these sources as wavy line or similar, transcribed here according to **L²**; fingering to note 1 from **J**, to note 10 from **L²**

Bar 6. **T**: variant to RH beats 1–6 difficult to read, but apparently consists of successive trills (*tr*), the first of which is imprecisely positioned above note 3 rather than note 4 as here; suggested realization as for ∿. (Compare the similar execution of the trills in Mozart, Sonata in D major K. 284 (205b), mvt 3, var. XI, bars 11, 30, 31; Sonata in C major K. 309 (284b), mvt 1, bars 51, 145.)

Bar 7. RH beats 1–3: despite their notational idiosyncrasies, the trills in the three variants will be played identically if the principal note *f²* is not repeated. **M²**: staccato to RH note 4 obviously omitted; here as in **F, G, E**, also bar 23.

Bars 8–9. **M²** adds '*p cresc.*' bar 8 beats 11–12 and, in consequence, removes *pp* bar 9 beat 9 while nevertheless retaining *p*

[17] For alternative interpretations of variants of this type see e.g. Paweł Kamiński, 'Identyfikacja ołówkowych dopisków Chopina w egzemplarzach pierwszych wydań z Biblioteki Uniwersyteckiej w Toruniu', *Muzyka*, 1 (2016), pp. 5–33.

bar 9 beat 1, even though it becomes redundant (hence its removal here)

Bar 10. **G, M¹,²**: probably redundant staccato dot to RH note 4; here no staccato dot (**F, E** as here). **M²**: no ♭ to *c¹* in LH chord 5, possibly an engraver's omission overlooked by Mikuli (cf. presence of flat sign in all other sources, including **M¹**); although this 'variant' results in less harmonic richness, it is retained here by way of contrast with the corresponding passage in bar 18. Note that in his recordings based on **M²** (Polydor 65786 (1920), Polydor 67246 (1936)), Mikuli's pupil Raoul Koczalski plays *cb¹* in LH chord 5.

Bars 11–12. **D**: '*8ᵛᵃ*' to bar 11 LH notes 7, 9 and bar 12 LH notes 1, 3 indicates doubling an octave below, not displacement of original note to lower octave (see comment to bar 16)

Bars 12, 20. See comments to original version

Bar 13. RH beat 1 (grace notes): same variant in **FR², J, S, SCHO**. Liaison from **D**.

Bar 15. **SCHO**: ending of trill on RH beat 3 as in **M²**. **M²**: staccato to RH note 6 obviously omitted (here as in **F, G, E**, also bar 23).

Bar 16. *Ossia* in **SCHO**:

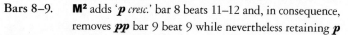

similar to variant to bar 24 from **K**.

T: '*8ᵛᵃ*' to LH note 7 indicates doubling an octave below, not displacement of original note to lower octave (see comment to bars 11–12).

Bar 18. Beats 10–12: ⟨ from **F, G, E**

Bars 18–20. **M¹**: '*poco ritard.*' at beginning of bar 18 (added by analogy to bar 10), then '*poco rall.*' bar 20 beats 8–12. **M²** retains former indication but replaces latter by 'zurückhaltend'. On the assumption that the '*poco ritard.*' is not authentic, it is not included here; instead, the '*poco rall.*' found in bar 20 in all sources except **M²** is reinstated.

Bar 21. RH beat 1 (grace notes): same variant in **FR², S, T, SCHO**. Liaison from **D**.

Bar 22. Variant from **T** possibly intended to start after *f♮²*; here after *e♮²* in order to avoid harmonic clash

Bar 23. RH beats 1–3 only: **SCHO** same variant as in **T**

Bar 24. **M², SCHO**: rhythm of RH chord 36 (upper note) and RH note 37, notated respectively as dotted semiquaver and demisemiquaver, corrected here to dotted demisemiquaver and hemidemisemiquaver. Variant from **K** (similar to *ossia* to bar 16 in **SCHO**): prolongation dot to note 4 (i.e. as in **G²**, in contrast to **F** and **E**, where it concerns note 3); incorrect barline before note 29.

Bars 25, 29. **M²**: lack of ♭ to *c¹* in LH chord 2 possibly an engraver's omission overlooked by Mikuli (cf. presence of ♭ in all other sources, including **M¹**); this 'variant' is retained here by way of contrast (major/minor) with bars 26 & 30. In his recordings (see comment to bar 10) Raoul Koczalski plays *c♮¹* in bar 25 LH chord 2 but *c♭¹* in bar 25 LH chord 5 and bar 29 LH chord 2.

Bar 26. See p. 13 n. 2 regarding variant after RH note 9 in cited exemplar of **F⁴**. Slur to last three RH notes by analogy with bar 27 RH notes 13–16.

Bar 27. **M²**: '*sempre cresc.*', as against '*sempre **pp***' in all other sources (including **M¹**). Two hypotheses are plausible:

1) In contrast to the original version, in which ***pp*** is retained throughout the preceding bar, Mikuli wanted a distinct reinforcement of the sonority here in order to differentiate it from the '*dolcissimo*' indicated just after. If that was indeed his intention, then putting '*sempre*' before '*cresc.*' was clumsy, given that such an indication would normally pertain to the continuation or reinforcement of a previous dynamic marking. In this particular context (bars 26–27), '*cresc.*' alone would suffice, although it would be necessary to add '*subito*' before the ensuing '*dolcissimo*'.

2) The '*cresc.*' was an engraving error overlooked by Mikuli. Here the second hypothesis is accepted, hence the restoration of '*sempre **pp***'. LH chord 12 (upper note): $a\natural^1$ in **M²** only; f^1 in other sources. In his recordings Raoul Koczalski plays f^1.

Bar 29. See comment to bars 25, 29

Bar 30. RH note 1 in **M²** has fingering '1', not the wedge staccato ('') found in all other sources (including **M¹**), nor fingering '5' (added by hand above '') in **D**, **S**. Here the '1' is retained in addition to the indispensable '', which indicates an essential lifting of the hand. **M²**: ***fz*** under RH chord 14, > above LH chord 9 (here ***fz*** ⏵ under RH chord 14, by analogy with long accent to RH note 14 in all other sources); redundant staccato dot to LH chord 12 (removed here by analogy with all other sources).

Bar 31. Variant from **S**: essential ♮ to RH note 7 missing. **W**: illegible variant positioned as per variant in **S**. **M²**: no g^1 in LH chord 6 (obvious omission); here as in all others sources. LH beats 10–12: erroneous notation in **M¹**  changed in **M²** to ; wedge staccato and original two-part voice-leading on beats 11, 12 as in **F**, **G**, **E** restored here.

Bar 32. **M²** (also Koczalski's recordings): last four RH notes semiquavers, not quavers as in all other sources. Fingering in RH variant from **L¹**, **ZR**: '5' to note 3 (in fact, to note 4 in original source, moved editorially here) from **ZR**; to notes 5–15 from both sources; to notes 16–19 from **L¹**. Variant in **L¹** differs from that in **ZR** by almost illegible ending in which LH part is not present. Repeated bb^1's in lower RH part at end of variant from **ZR** could be harmonically enriched as follows:

LH variant from **T**, **W**, **X**: notes 10–13 (indicated in **W** by vertical strokes only) added just after the printed text, thus changing the original sequence of RH/LH attacks. In the context of the *senza tempo*, it would also be possible to play the extended LH figure in the variant less broadly, i.e. confining it only to beats 1–6. Fingering to notes 1, 2 from **T**, **X**, and to notes 5, 6 from **X**; extension of slur for LH notes 9–13 from **X**.

W: the initial version of the variant at the end of the cadenza was as follows:

It was then modified by crossing out the *ottava* sign as well as LH notes 2–5, thereby creating a sort of echo of the same figuration at the beginning of the cadenza. A similar if reduced version of this figuration appears at the end of the variant in **T**, and the left hand is also present (if briefly) at the end of the variant in **ZR**. The existence of both counterparts lends further authority to the corresponding variant in **W**.

Bars 33–34. **M²**: no pedalling in bar 33 (obvious omission), open pedal in bar 34; here open pedal in bar 33, as in all other sources (including **M¹**)

Bar 34. Variant from **W**, apparently limited to just one bar, meshes with bar 35 in variants from **L¹**, **S**, **ZR** and **T**

Bars 34–35. **M²**, **SCHO**: bar 34 last RH note, bar 35 RH note 1 g^4 – possibly an engraving error overlooked by Mikuli (also Scholtz); this 'variant' is retained here despite presence of eb^4 in variants **L¹**, **S**, **T**, **ZR**. In his recordings Raoul Koczalski plays g^4. Variant from **L¹**, **S**, **ZR**: fingering to bar 34 LH notes 1, 2 from **L¹**, **S**; to bar 34 LH notes 3–5 from **L¹**; to bar 34 RH note 5 bar 34 from **S**, **ZR**; to bar 35 note 1 bar 35 from **S**. Bar 35 RH note 1 notated as 𝄐♩· in **L¹**, **T**; as 𝄐𝅝· in **S**; as 𝄐♩· in **ZR**.

Variant from **T**: imprecisely notated 8va encompasses last two notes in bar 34; here 8va only to bar 35 RH note 1 (similar variant from **L¹**, **S**, **ZR** as here).

The Oxford Original Edition (edited by Edouard Ganche and published in 1932) suggests the following transcription of the variant from **S** (omitting the *ottava* in bar 35):